The New Work Order

Behind the Language of the New Capitalism

James Paul Gee, Glynda Hull
and Colin Lankshear

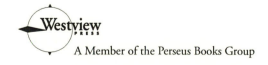

A Member of the Perseus Books Group

First published in Sydney, Australia 1996 by
Allen & Unwin Pty Ltd
9 Atchison Street, St Leonards, NSW 2065
Phone: (61 2) 9901 4088
Fax: (61 2) 9906 2218
E-mail: 100252.103@compuserve.com

Published in 1996 in the United States of America by
Westview Press, a member of the Perseus Books Group

Library of Congress Cataloging-in-Publication
Data available upon request

Set in 10/12 Times by DOCUPRO, Sydney

10 9 8

The New Work Order

Behind the Language of the
New Capitalism

Contents

*To Samuel James Gee who was born
while this book was being written.*

Acknowledgments

I am grateful to the following who have responded to, or inspired, my work on language, literacy, and the new capitalism—though they need bear no blame for its shortcomings: Courtney Cazden, Bill Cope, Norman Fairclough, Ian Falk, Aviva Freedman, Peter Freebody, Mary Kalantzis, Gunther Kress, Jay Lemke, Carmen Luke, Allan Luke, Peter Medway, Sarah Michaels, Martin Nakata, Peter O'Connor, Hugh (Bud) Mehan and Jim Wertsch.

James Paul Gee

Special thanks to the graduate students and research partners par excellence whose work made the Silicon Valley chapters possible: Meg Gebhard, Mark Jury, Mira Katz, and Oren Ziv. Sincere thanks as well to the US agencies whose funding supported this research: the Spencer Foundation, the National Center for Research in Vocational Education, and the National Center for Research in Writing and Literacy. W. Norton Grubb and Sarah Warshauer Freedman lead these two research centers at Berkeley: much gratitude is due them for their long-term interest and guidance.

Glynda Hull

My thanks to Allan Levett for stimulating my interest in the new global economy, to the New Zealand Qualifications Authority for supporting allied research during 1992, and to QUT's Faculty of Education and members of its Adult and Workplace Education working party for helping put many ideas into everyday perspective. My enduring esteem, appreciation, and cariño goes to my lifefriends in Monte Fresco, from whom I have acquired and learned more than anyone could reasonably expect from an education—even in the school of life.

Colin Lankshear

Preface

Change is a leading motif of our times. A new world is being born, dominated by a new global capitalism sometimes called post-capitalism now that visible socialist alternatives appear to have collapsed. It is a world fuelled by fiercer competition than ever before and by unprecedented high technology. It is a world, too, that ought to concern all of us, not just those in business or concerned with economics. And so we three—all people primarily concerned with language, learning, and literacy—turn our attention here to the 'new work order' of the new capitalism. In the pages that follow we investigate the new work order and how it impacts on the social practices of language, learning and literacy—and they on it. We look at how human lives, human identities, and human possibilities are shaped and circumscribed within our distinctly new times. And we ask how education may help prepare us for tackling the deep challenges and problems generated by the new capitalism.

Before we say why we wrote this book and who we hope reads it, let us turn briefly to the question: How did this new world come to be? The short account (Madrick 1995) is this. Starting in the nineteenth century, and going well into the twentieth, the United States built itself into the world's dominant economic power thanks to its space and natural resources, its huge internal market, its mastery of mass production, and its growing global power. After World War II other 'developed' countries began for the first time to compete seriously with the United States, using its own favored methods, namely standardization and mass production. Increasingly, however, fierce competition for markets and, yet more importantly, scientific and technological advances led to the fragmentation of the mass market into a myriad of sub-markets or niche markets.

Technological changes allowed goods to be 'customized' while still being produced in large numbers—that is, to be dovetailed into the (often newly created) identities of specific types of consumers. And there was no shortage of competitors wanting to create and enter these niche markets as a new form of competitive advantage. In the act, they initiated the decline of the mass market and the business strategies that went with it. So-called 'mass customization' loses some of the advantages of scope (of the market) and scale (of production) of the old mass market and leads, after a while, to less or at least harder earned profit. At the same time, social, political, and technological changes allowed far more people and countries to compete with each other for the same jobs and the same markets. Finally, increased information has allowed consumers, at least in the developed world, to take full advantage of the competition, driving each competitor to produce the highest quality for the best price, or see their business go elsewhere. In the end, the big (mass market) pie—formerly controlled by the United States—has been cut into ever smaller pieces with ever fiercer competition over each piece.

The results of all this? We will see a good many in this book. They include more stressful and more responsible work for those who have 'good' jobs, a proliferation of low-paying and temporary jobs, and many people with no jobs. They include a widening gap between the poor and the rich. They include a world in which national borders—and the concerns of our fellow 'citizens' in need—are considered to matter less and less. They include a world in which there are often a small number of big winners and a large number of losers in the race for jobs, wealth, and markets (Frank and Cook 1995). They include as well the promise—amid these perils—of more meaningful work, the valuing of diversity, the dispersal of centralized authority and hegemony, and the wider distribution of knowledge within and across local 'communities of practice'.

So, why write this book? The three authors share an allegiance to a *sociocultural* approach to language, learning, and literacy, believing that these practices can be understood only when they are situated within their social, cultural, and historical contexts. When they are so situated, it becomes clear that they are always and everywhere connected to *social identities*, that is, to different kinds of 'people'. In basic terms, 'people like us' do things, say things, learn and know things, so as, precisely, to be 'people like us'. Human beings are all—each of us—many different 'kinds of people' in different contexts: different kinds of men and women, different kinds of African-

Americans or Asian-Americans, different kinds of Australians or 'Brits' or Costa Ricans, different kinds of students and teachers, different kinds of working class or middle class people, different kinds of workers and bosses. What's more, other people, and the social institutions they embody, often want us, sometimes pressure us and at times force us to be other kinds, different kinds, new kinds of people.

In our view the new work order is largely about trying to create new social identities or new kinds of people: new leaders, new workers, new students, new teachers, new citizens, new communities, even new 'private' people who are supposed to dissolve the separation between their lives outside work and their lives inside it. Since the three of us share an interest in how language, learning, and literacy get caught up in social practices to produce and reproduce social identities, with their accompanying interests and values, the new work order provides a tailor-made focus around which to explore and develop this shared interest.

We hope that this book helps to bring together two different kinds of readers: people interested in language, learning, and literacy who may be beginning to think about work and business as central and not peripheral to their concerns; and people already well grounded in business and work who want to see their issues in a wider context, one that makes their concerns a central focus of educational and socio-cultural theories and practices.

To give you a sense of what we are talking about in a more concrete way, we will use a brief example (see also Gee 1993). In a now classic article published in the *Harvard Business Review* in 1990 William Wiggenhorn, the corporate vice-president for training and education at Motorola, described Motorola's commitment to 'Total Quality Control', one of a plethora of movements and techniques advocated for business reform. Motorola has implemented a massive education program— Motorola University—to apprentice its workers to the new perspective.

Motorola's corporate goal was to achieve a standard of quality that Wiggenhorn, following statisticians and industrial engineers, calls 'Six Sigma'. Six Sigma means 'six standard deviations from a statistical performance average'—or, as Wiggenhorn goes on to say:

> In plain English, Six Sigma translates into 3.4 defects per million
> opportunities, or production that is 99.99966% defect free. (By
> contrast, and according to formulas not worth explaining here, 5
> [sigma] is 233 defects per million, and 4 [sigma] is 6210. Airlines
> achieve 6.5 [sigma] in safety—counting fatalities as defects—but only
> 3.5 to 4 [sigma] in baggage handling. Doctors and pharmacists achieve

an accuracy of just under 5 [sigma] in writing and filling prescriptions. (Wiggenhorn 1990: 74):

Applied to the chef in the cafeteria, Wiggenhorn says, this goal would mean 'he can burn five muffins this year, two muffins next year, and eventually none at all'. Wiggenhorn is well aware, as he says, that Six Sigma applied to muffins is 'in one sense a fiction'. He further acknowledges that 'if we presented it to the chef as an ultimatum, it would also be insulting'. The real point, he says, is that

> . . . importing that quality language from manufacturing to the rest of the company stimulates a kind of discussion we might not otherwise have had. It also tells people they're important, since the time-cycle and quality standards so vital to manufacturing and product design now also apply to the chef, the security guard, and the clerical support people.
>   What we actually said to the chef was that he made a consistently Six Sigma chocolate chip cookie—in my opinion it ranks with the best in the world—and we wanted him to do the same with muffins. He said, 'The reason I can't make a better muffin is that you don't trust me with the key to the freezer. I have to make the batter the night before because when I get here in the mornings the makings are still locked up. When batter sits for 12 hours, it's never as good as batter you make fresh and pop directly in the oven.' He was right, of course. The language of quality can also be used to talk about trust (Wiggenhorn 1990: 74).

Wiggenhorn starts with a *technical tool* (a particular type of statistics) and moves to a *culture* (trust) through a *social intervention* (changing the relationships and role of the chef). This progression is, in fact, typical of much of the new capitalism. A business adopts a set of tools and procedures, often based on a new reform emanating from consultants or business schools, designed to change social relations in the workplace (a form of sociotechnical engineering) and thereby create a new workplace culture or new workplace 'core values'.

Wiggenhorn starts with the highly technical subject of 'sigma statistics', but then quickly assures us that these matters can be translated into 'plain English', albeit a 'plain English' in which, all of a sudden, human fatalities become a 'defect' (in the quality of life?). We get, perhaps, a new form of fetishism, not Marx's 'commodity fetishism' but 'quality fetishism': deaths, prescriptions, and baggage are equated, since they can all be ranged on a scale of quality (rather than, as in classical commodity fetishism, on a scale of money). Wiggenhorn's text is making things *happen* to language and people.

He is concerned with new ways of acting, taking, thinking, valuing, and being in the workplace.

Wiggenhorn moves on to apply his technical 'sigma talk' to the chef, actively translating the chef and his muffins from worker and objects in the old industrial capitalism into partner and quality product in the new 'fast capitalism'. But the translation also involves changing the technical talk that encapsulates the theory into the more 'humane' talk that is directed to the chef in practice.

As a formal tool the sigma talk is meant to set the *goals* of the organization as a whole and all its parts by giving a measure of productivity, where productivity is now defined as 'total quality' for the customer and not, any longer, in terms of quantity of production or (at least directly) in terms of (short-term) profit. However, when a formal tool like the sigma language is applied to individuals, and not at the level of the organization and its goals, it needs to be retranslated. It must now be transformed into a sociotechnical device, a social intervention, for creating and sustaining new social relationships among leaders (managers), workers, *and* things (like machines and muffins).

For the purposes of social intervention the sigma talk is translated into language and practices that help the chef 'join up and join into' the new quality culture of the organization defined in the first instance by the vision and goals objectified (in part) by the sigma talk in its formal guise. This dual coding (as formal tool and social intervention) is the reason that it is only *in one sense* a fiction to apply Six Sigma to muffins. As a formal tool it is no fiction at all, but as a sociotechnical device it needs to be made into more 'humane' interaction commensurate with quality culture: presented 'as such' it would be insulting.

But now we face a core paradox in the new capitalism: the very language that objectifies the ends, goals, and vision of the organization, and which thus underlies the culture of the organization, is *insulting* if spoken directly to the workers/partners. The new capitalism stresses fully informed workers who actively participate in the quality culture of the organization and have (and take) full responsibility for all the organizational ramifications of the jobs they do. This is what is meant by 'empowerment'.

And yet the very language that encapsulates the ends, goals, and vision of the organization and its culture must be translated into a language of social intervention or manipulation (depending on the view you take of the matter) so as not to insult the workers/partners and so as to motivate them. But, then, the 'trust' that is instilled in the worker is based on forces from the outside, not on *real* participation in the language and practices that objectify the ends, goals, and vision of the organization, which are still the preserve of an elite priesthood of leaders (managers) and consultants.

The paradox is deeper yet: the newly empowered and newly 'critical thinking' workers cannot really question the goals, visions, and values that define the very parameters of the new capitalist business in the new global work order. Such questioning might well mean exiting the new capitalist world and seeking employment in Third World-like, low-wage, marginal jobs in the remaining backwaters of the old capitalism, or having no employment at all (Reich 1992). The worker's 'freedom' is fixed within the margins of the goals, ends, and vision set by the new capitalism and its theoreticians. The problem can be put another way: real commitment and belief, as well as real learning, require that learners be able to engage in genuine dialogue and contestation with viewpoints, but such genuine contestation is ultimately problematic in a business setting where, in the end, profit is the goal and the competition is at one's heels.

While it may sound as though we are criticizing the new capitalism from the outside, the paradox to which we are pointing here is readily acknowledged by business people themselves. It is, in fact, as we will see in this book, one of the major hurdles of actualizing the new work order. Whether one wants to hasten the coming of the new work order or to stop it—or to transform it into something else—it is a paradox that will figure centrally in anyone's theories about, and practices in our new times.

Though Total Quality Control (e.g., Sashkin & Kiser 1993) is but one approach among many, and in some respects a bit *passé* amid the ever changing 'flavor of the month' business reforms, it nicely captures what is really at stake in the new work order: new kinds of people engaged in new social practices. And where there are new kinds of people and new social practices, those of us interested in how language, learning, and literacy work in context—and how they relate to values, politics, and power—will find fertile fields indeed.

This book comprises two parts which we intend to speak back and forth to each other. The first three chapters take up the new work order in 'theory', the next three chapters take it up in 'practice'. However, this divide is somewhat arbitrary: there is plenty of theory in the practice and practice in the theory, and each set of chapters repeatedly appeals to insights offered in the other set. We have attempted to write the book throughout with one voice, though readers will see distinctive traces of the different authors here and there.

The first chapter—Sociocultural literacy, discourses, and the new work order—introduces a particular approach to situating language, literacy, and learning within their social and cultural contexts with due respect to the workings of values and power. We here first make contact with the new capitalism and argue that it should be seen as a crucial additional context within which to understand the workings of language, literacy, and learning—and thus a crucial concern for people in sociocultural literacy studies.

The second chapter—Fast capitalism: theory and practice—is a primer, with accompanying critical discussion, of the 'theoretical' apparatus behind the new capitalism, namely the myriad of books and articles written to shape or reshape its coming into being. We call the versions of the new work order advocated in this literature 'fast capitalism', so as to distinguish a set of texts about the new capitalism from the phenomenon itself which is unfolding in actual workplaces.

The third chapter—'Alignments: education and the new capitalism'—broadens the picture, placing the themes and practices of the new capitalism within the context of broader intellectual movements affecting many disciplines and spheres of life. This chapter also argues that, within the parameters of this larger picture, there is a growing alignment between school reformers and reforms and the desires and needs of the new capitalism, both in theory and in practice. The chapter closes by arguing that there is also a growing convergence—in words, if not deeds—between the new capitalism and traditional critics of capitalism.

The fourth chapter begins the case study part of the book. Chapters 4 and 5—'A tale of one factory'—go together. They deal in detail, using ethnographic methods, with a new-capitalist workplace in the United States that is implementing a major workplace reform, namely self-directed work teams. Such teams represent, as becomes clear in the first three chapters, many of the major motifs of the new capitalism. Chapter 4 deals with training classes intended to prepare workers—in heart, mind, and body—for operating in the teams, and takes up key issues of education in relation to new-capitalist workplaces. Chapter 5 deals with the teams in practice, looking closely at their conversational and social interactions. It places a good many of the issues discussed throughout this book in actual settings and practices. The reality 'on the ground' is often much more complex than the theories in the books might imply.

Chapter 6—'A tale of one village: global capitalism and Nicaragua'—takes us out of the context of the so-called developed world and into the Third World and the emerging Fourth World of the new capitalism. This chapter is a case study of the people in one work cooperative in a village in Nicaragua, struggling to survive as they are buffeted by the waves of the global capitalism. Their struggles speak volumes about the perils and possibilities of our 'new times'.

We conclude the book with no final answers or big solutions but with some possibilities that we believe merit considering and discussing. The book as a whole is intended to encourage readers to confront complex problems and to construct their own broader theories, critiques, and practices fit for a new world in which things change and 'the center cannot hold'. We can only begin here to consider what beast it is that 'slouches toward Bethlehem'.

1 Sociocultural literacy, discourses, and the new work order

A sociocultural approach involves the view that language, literacy, and learning can only be understood when situated in their social and cultural settings. This book argues that we have to go a step further: they need to be situated, as well, in the context of society's 'work order'. This is particularly crucial as we enter into a new work order within a new capitalism. In this chapter we develop a sociocultural approach to language, literacy, and learning that deals directly with this new work order and that integrates concern for schools with concern for workplaces.

I   A sociocultural approach

On the traditional view, literacy is seen as a largely *psychological* ability—something true about our heads. We, on the other hand, see literacy as a matter of *social practices*—something to do with social, institutional, and cultural relationships (e.g., Gee 1996; Heath 1983; Kress 1985; Lankshear with Lawler 1987; Scollon and Scollon 1981; Street 1984; for related work from the perspective of social cognition see Lave and Wenger 1991).

To show you how we arrive at this claim we need to run through a simple argument (Gee 1996). The argument is meant to show that social, institutional, and cultural relationships play a much more prominent role in literacy than one might have thought. We will sketch the argument in relation to *reading*. (There is an obvious analogue of the argument that concerns *writing*, rather than reading.)

The argument begins as follows: Whatever literacy is, it must have something to do with *reading*. And *reading* is always *reading some-*

1

thing. Furthermore, if one has not *understood* what one has read then one has not read it. So reading is always reading *something* with *understanding*. Now, this something that one reads with understanding is always a text of a *certain type* which is read in a *certain way*. The text might be a comic book, a novel, a poem, a legal brief, a technical manual, a textbook in physics, a newspaper article, an essay in the social sciences or philosophy, a 'self-help' book, a recipe, and so forth through many different types of text. Each of these different types of text requires somewhat different background knowledge and somewhat different skills.

In fact, all of us can read certain types of text and not others. If any highly educated people need convincing of this point, and assuming they have had no background in philosophy, they need only read a few pages of Hegel's *Phenomenology of Mind*. They will immediately become convinced that they cannot read Hegel in any useful sense of the word 'read'.

Furthermore, any text can be read in *different ways*. Here we need an example. Consider the following sentences from a brief story in which a man named Gregory has wronged his former girlfriend Abigail: 'Heartsick and dejected, Abigail turned to Slug with her tale of woe. Slug, feeling compassion for Abigail, sought out Gregory and beat him brutally'.

In one study (Gee 1989, 1996) some readers, who happened to be African-Americans, claimed that these sentences 'say' that Abigail told Slug to beat up Gregory. On the other hand, other readers, who happened not to be African-Americans, claimed that these sentences 'say' no such thing. These readers subseqently claimed, in fact, that the African-Americans had *misread* the sentences. The African-Americans responded: 'If you turn to someone with a tale of woe and, in particular, someone named 'Slug', you are most certainly asking him to *do* something in the way of violence and you are most certainly responsible when he's done it'.

The point is that these different people read the sentences in different ways and thought that others had read them in the 'wrong' ways. Even if we think that the African-Americans—or the others— have read the sentences incorrectly, the very act of claiming that their reading is incorrect admits that there is a *way* to read the sentences and that we can dispute how the sentences ought to be read (and we can ask *who* determines the 'ought' and why). If we say that the African-Americans have gone too far beyond the text—or the others not far enough—we are still conceding that there is an issue of 'how far' to go and what counts as *a* way (or *the* way) of reading a text.

Now we have made out the case that *reading* is *understanding* a particular *type of text* in a *certain way*. All of us can read certain texts in certain ways and not others. Reading is thus a *plural* notion: *readings*, rather than *reading*.

The next stage of the argument asks: *How* does one acquire the ability to read a certain type of text in a certain way? Here the sociocultural approach argues that the literature on the acquisition and development of literacy is clear: a way of reading a certain type of text is acquired *only* when it is acquired in a 'fluent' or 'native-like' way, by one's being embedded in (apprenticed as a member of) a *social practice* wherein people not only *read* texts of this type in this way but also *talk* about such texts in certain ways, *hold certain attitudes and values* about them, and *socially interact* over them in certain ways (Garton & Pratt 1989; Heath 1983; John-Steiner, Panofsky & Smith 1994; Scollon & Scollon 1981; Lave & Wenger 1991).

Texts are parts of *lived, talked, enacted, value-and-belief-laden* practices carried out in specific places and at specific times. Think of legal texts, comic books, recipes, Dick-and-Jane readers, basal readers, graffiti, traffic tickets, lab notebooks, journal articles, notes to family members, manuals, and so forth. You feel your mind run through quite different practices, quite different configurations of people, actions, and settings, quite different 'ways of being in the world' at a time and place.

Now it turns out, to move to the next and last stage of our argument, that in these social practices we can never extract just the bits concerned with reading (or 'literacy' in any other sense) and ignore all the bits concerned with talk, action, interaction, attitudes, values, objects, tools, and spaces. *All the bits*—the print bits and the non-print bits—constitute an integral whole. Apart from the social practices in which they are acquired and in which they are always embedded, the 'literacy bits' do not exist, or at least they do not mean anything (in several senses of the word 'mean'). Once extracted from the practices they are not the 'same thing' that existed in the living social practice.

That's the end of the argument. We start from reading and arrive at social practices integrating talk, action, interaction, beliefs, and values. We arrive at specific and diverse *ways of being in the world*. Let us return to the sentences from the story about Gregory, Abigail, and Slug. The African-Americans read, on this occasion, out of a social practice that treats written texts as if they *say* things the way people do. In this sort of practice, written texts get their meanings in the way speakers do—by embedding their words within the contexts, conditions, and constraints of experiences one has had in the world. In this sort of practice you just don't turn to a guy named 'Slug' with your problems and then claim you're blameless when he beats someone up. You cannot evade responsibility by hiding behind the 'literal meanings' of words.

The others in Gee's study read, on the same occasion, out of a social practice that treats texts as though they have 'explicit' and socially invariable meanings all by themselves, sitting there on the page, quite apart from experiences one has actually had. These meanings follow 'logically' from socially invariable and mentally stored reading skills. Here, too, this way of reading is deeply connected to specific ways of talking, acting, interacting, valuing, and being in the world; ways that are, in fact, quite pervasive in many school-based social practices.

On this occasion the others chose to read out of school-like social practices; on other occasions they might not have. So too the African-Americans could have, on a different occasion, read out of different social practices, connected to different social identities. What one cannot do is read out of *no* social practice. There are many 'ways of being in the world', connected to work, social groups, cultures, institutions, and communities with different interests and values. And, in the context of the new work order, many of these are rapidly changing.

Reading and writing always swim in a far richer sea than traditional approaches to literacy allow for. As things like telecommunications, computers, graphics, virtual reality, and cyberspace become progressively more central, our basic point doesn't change. These too are elements in, bits and pieces of, social practices—not 'stand alone' realities.

When we take a sociocultural approach to literacy we exit the mind and ultimately the school, and enter the world, including the world of work. In a sociocultural approach, the focus of learning and education is not children, nor schools, but human lives seen as *trajectories* through multiple social practices in various social institutions. If learning is to be efficacious, then what a child or adult does *now* as a learner must be connected in meaningful and motivating ways with 'mature' (insider) versions of related social practices.

Educators have for too long given pride of place to children and schools, to the detriment of both. However, this conclusion does not emerge only from a sociocultural approach to language and literacy. It is a leitmotif of writing on the new work order in the new capitalism (which we discuss further in Section III below, and in detail in Chapter 2). The argument here is that the world has changed and the nature of learning and knowledge is changing along with it (Aronowitz & DiFazio 1994; Drucker 1993; Handy 1989; Kelly 1994; Kennedy 1993; Kotter 1995; Lash & Urry 1994; Reich 1992; Smith 1995).

Knowledge now goes out of date too fast to rely on what you have learned in school, including college. Furthermore, 'academic', 'specialist' knowledge—the sort that has traditionally been seen as the highest goal of good schooling, at least for those who are college or university bound—is deeply problematic amid the complex systems of our contemporary and fast-changing world. For example, listen to Peter Senge, who has championed *learning organizations*:

> The 'compartmentalization of knowledge' creates a false sense of confidence. For example, the traditional disciplines that influence management—such disciplines as economics, accounting, marketing, and psychology—divide the world into neat subdivisions within which one can often say, 'This is the problem and here is the solution'. But the boundaries that make the subdivisions are fundamentally arbitrary—as any manager finds out who attempts to treat an important problem as if it is purely 'an economic problem' or 'an accounting problem'. Life comes to us whole. It is only the analytic lens we impose that makes it seem as if problems can be isolated and solved. When we forget that it is 'only a lens,' we lose the spirit of openness (Senge 1991: 283).

The business world, as part and parcel of massive global economic, technological, and social change, now sees *knowledge* as its primary 'value'. Contemporary, globally competitive businesses don't any longer really compete on the basis of their products or services *per se*. They compete, rather, on the basis of how much learning and knowledge they can use as leverage in order to expeditiously invent, produce, distribute and market their goods and services, as well as to innovatively vary and customize them. Such knowledge is made up of both highly technical components and components dealing with communication, motivation, and social interaction. Similar changes are affecting non-business institutions as well.

'Knowledge' used to be the purview of schools and universities, who had 'rights' over what counted as knowledge. Given the emphasis in the new business world on knowledge work and knowledge workers, the nature of schools and universities is implicated at the very heart

of this world. The new work order puts a huge stress on the need for
lifelong learning and the need continually to adapt, change, and learn
new skills, very often *on site* while carrying out the job.

Schools and universities, especially as they are currently structured,
no longer have a monopoly on learning, and indeed are not always
well suited to the task:

> 'In a knowledge age economy,' Louis Perelman writes in *School's
> Out*, 'the learning enterprise is strategically crucial.' 'Far too crucial
> to leave to the schools', he adds. Perelman . . . imagines all the
> world turned into a giant learning network . . . The guiding
> principle is personal learning 'on demand', 'just in time', 'whenever
> and however the opportunity is wanted' . . .
>
> At one point, Perelman admiringly cites Harvard's Professor
> Shoshana Zuboff, who reports working with a plant manager in an
> advanced manufacturing operation 'who was toying with the idea of
> calling the plant a college [because] . . . work and learning [there]
> had become increasingly interconnected' (Peters 1994: 183–184,
> 185; see also Perelman 1992).

The bottom line is this: the focus of education, we argue, should
be on *social practices* and their connections across various social and
cultural sites and institutions. Learners should be viewed as lifelong
trajectories through these sites and institutions, as *stories* with multiple
twists and turns. What we say about their beginnings should be shaped
by what we intend to say about their middles and ends, and vice versa.
As *their* stories are rapidly and radically changing, we need to change
our stories about skills, learning, and knowledge. Our focus, as well,
should be on multiple learning sites and their rich and complex interconnections. We will see below and in other chapters that this focus
on social practices brings us squarely up against the growing concern
in the new capitalism with *sociotechnical practices*—that is, with the
design of technology and social relations within the workplace to
facilitate productivity and commitment, sometimes in highly 'indoctrinating' ways.

In the end we need to see learning and knowledge as distributed
across lifetimes, social practices, social groupings, and institutions. We
can and should ask how much knowledge resides in a family, an
organization, a social practice, a particular technology, a community, a
culture, or a nation—not just in a person's head. We can and should
ask, also, how this knowledge is exploited for good or ill.

Knowledge, then, is like *potential energy* in physics, energy that
can be released in various forms and for various purposes. Knowledge

is energy that resides in individuals, groups, practices, technologies, communities, organizations, and nations. We can define knowledge, like physical energy, in terms of the amount of *work* that it can be used to produce. But we badly need to reconceptualize what work is or should be in our changing world. Schools and children are only one element in this much bigger picture.

Furthermore, the new business world is offering education new challenges. For example, as we discuss further below, many businesses, in the face of the new global hypercompetition of our science-and-technology-driven world, are seeking to break down the barriers between work, community, and private life. They seek and demand total commitment and full immersion in the goals, vision, and practices of the organization (Boyett & Conn 1992; Peters 1992; Smith 1995).

Work in the old capitalism was alienating. Workers were forced to sell their labor, but often with little mental, emotional, or social investment in the business. Today they are asked to invest their hearts, minds, and bodies fully in their work. They are asked to think and act critically, reflectively, and creatively. While this offers a less alienating view of work and labor, in practice it can also amount to a form of mind control and high-tech, but indirect coercion.

Such promises and such perils ought, we believe, to become a central focus of sociocultural approaches to literacy and educational theory generally. This is all the more true as schools, under the aegis of school reform, become progressively more influenced by new capitalist businesses and their views about learning (a matter we discuss in Chapter 3).

II   A case study concerning schools and workplaces

We want now to argue the relevance of a sociocultural approach for an *integrated* view of learning—one applicable to children and adults, to schools as well as workplaces. To accomplish this we look at one specific case, one that shares features with schools and workplaces. Our case concerns the nature of literacy in law schools in the United States. Of course, law school is a form of schooling, but it is also training for a specific form of work. Law school, we will argue, is typical of much learning in both reforming schools and new workplaces—and it reflects, as we will see, some of the key debates in education today. Thus our case study of law school is meant to be an exemplary tale. Our discussion will also allow us to introduce the notion of 'Discourses', a notion we will use at various points in this book. What is important about the typical US law school for us is that it is a paradigm example of how people learn and become socialized within social practices—an approach more and more being advocated in schools and in the world of work.

Our discussion is based on the work of Monique Minnis (1994). Minnis claims that success in law school depends on specialized literacy skills which law professors typically *do not overtly teach*. And she points out that many minority students face deep difficulties in attempting to acquire these specialized skills.

In the typical US law school, instruction in the first year involves total immersion in the course material. Teachers do not lecture in class, rather they engage in adversarial interactions with students patterned after those of judge and lawyer in appellate courtrooms. The dominant instructional approach is the 'case method'. This method consists of discussing and comparing appellate opinions through a question-and-answer routine sometimes called 'Socratic dialogue':

> Before every class meeting, students are expected to have read and briefed, or summarized in writing, several appellate opinions from a book containing pivotal case law on the course topic. When called on in class, students must be prepared to review and analyze specific opinions, compare the details of several opinions, and explain how the opinions might have been rendered differently.
>
> The burden of divining pattern in the entire body of cases is on the students. Typically the professor's role is to expose, in the students' presentations, the hazards of ignoring alternative interpretations of the case material. Students are advised to be alert and ready to duck or strike lest their adversary, the professor, catch them off guard. In other words, law school classes, much like those in the martial arts, are run as a kind of contest between opponents. Always, discussion in such classes is exegetical; it is anchored in *texts*, in written accounts and judgments of past events (Minnis 1994: 352–53).

To write a competent brief the student has to be able to read the text being dealt with in much the same way as the professor does. Student readers must know how such texts are structured. They must know, for example how sentence structure is used to signal emphasis, importance, and other communicative effects. They must also see 'some statements as relatively general (or relatively specific) renderings of others, some ideas and discussions as subparts of others, and the whole of an exposition as integrated by an organizing idea' (356). And they must do this in order ultimately to see and be able to summarize the argument that the text propounds.

Students are not taught these reading skills—the ones necessary for them to be able to write briefs—directly. Briefs are not, for instance, turned in to the professor; they are written for the students' own use in class. 'The feedback students receive on their briefs is provided indirectly and to everyone at once, through analysis of the briefed cases in class' (357). This sort of indirect feedback is quite unlikely to involve overt attention to structural patterns and writing conventions, let alone reading conventions. Nonetheless, these must be 'picked up', along with (and actually as part and parcel of) concepts, values, and ways of interacting that are specific to the legal domain.

In law school, then, the traditional instructional methods do not describe or explicate procedures (like writing briefs, engaging in legal argumentation, or reading legal texts). Rather they *employ* these procedures publicly. So a key point here is that instruction 'occurs *inside* the procedure; it is not *about* the procedure, its rationale, its powers, or its limitations' (361). This is why law school *works*; it is also why it *excludes* certain sorts of people.

One of the basic assumptions of law school is that if students are not told overtly what to do and how to proceed, this will spur them on essentially to teach themselves. Minnis argues that this assumption does not, however, work equally well for everyone. Many students from minority or otherwise non-mainstream backgrounds fail in law school.

Minnis argues that this is so because these students have not, in their prior schooling and social experience, been exposed to and coached in the sorts of competitive academic behaviors and 'other survival skills appropriate to the situation encountered in the law school classroom' (362).

Contemporary legal education is designed for the good students, those who can understand what the professors mean but never explicitly say in the classes. Not surprisingly, given that mutual unspoken understanding between teachers and students requires common prior experiences, most good law students are traditional law students. They are students whose economic, social, and educational backgrounds are much like those of traditional law professors. These students, that is, are members of middle- and upper-class society, the dominant culture, the culture that shaped the law. Accordingly, they are inclined to accept without question beliefs that are characteristic of that culture and that give them an advantage in law school. In short, their personal histories have taught them to confront the world aggressively; they esteem reasoning over other ways of knowing, individual accomplishment over collective accomplishment, and competition over cooperation (Minnis 1994: 380).

It must be stressed, however, that the problem is *not just* that non-mainstream students have not had the same sorts of educational preparation as those who take more 'naturally' to law school instruction. To see what more is at stake we need to introduce the notion of Discourses.

Law school is a set of related social practices. We say that such related social practices constitute a Discourse (with a capital 'D' to distinguish it from 'discourse', which means 'a stretch of spoken or written language' or 'language in use'). So, there is a 'law school Discourse', which is of course connected to the larger Discourse of the law.

A Discourse is composed of ways of talking, listening, reading, writing, acting, interacting, believing, valuing, and using tools and objects, in particular settings and at specific times, so as to display or to recognize a particular social identity. Law school teachers and students enact specific social identities or 'social positions' in the Discourse of law school. The Discourse creates social positions (or perspectives) from which people are 'invited' ('summoned') to speak, listen, act, read and write, think, feel, believe and value in certain characteristic, historically recognizable ways, in combination with their own individual style and creativity (Bourdieu 1979/1984, 1991; Foucault 1980).

There are innumerable Discourses in modern societies: different sorts of street gangs, elementary schools and classrooms, academic disciplines and their sub-specialities, police, birdwatchers, ethnic groups, genders, executives, feminists, social classes and sub-classes, and so on and so forth. Each is composed of some set of related social practices and social identities (or 'positions'). Each Discourse contracts complex relations of complicity, tension, and opposition with other Discourses.

Another way to put the matter is this: Discourses create, produce, and reproduce opportunities for people to be and recognize certain *kinds of people* (Hacking 1986, 1994). We are all capable of being different kinds of people in different Discourses. We are all capable of being new kinds of people. There are kinds of policemen; kinds of African-Americans; kinds of Americans; kinds of men and kinds of women; kinds of lawyers and doctors; kinds of street gang members; kinds of students (in kinds of schools). Discourses, at particular historical junctures, in complicity and tension with each other, create and constrain what these kinds can be by producing and reproducing the possibilities of how they are enacted and recognized. In fact, we argue in this book that new kinds of learners, students, citizens, leaders, and workers are being created as we speak by the new capitalism.

Now, back to the law. The moral is this: the social practices and positions of the law school Discourse conflict, and conflict seriously, with the social practices and positions of the other Discourses to which many minorities and other non-mainstream students belong. They conflict much less—or not at all—with the social practices and positions of the other Discourses to which many mainstream students belong.

Let us put the matter somewhat differently. The Discourse of law school creates *kinds of people* who (overtly or tacitly) define themselves as different from—often better than—other *kinds of people*. For many minority and other non-mainstream students the Discourse of law school makes them be *both* kinds of people. They get to define their kind (as law student) as different from—often better than—their own kind (as a member of one of their other Discourses). A paradox indeed—unfortunately one they get to live and feel in their bodies and their minds.

Let us give a specific example of how these differences can work out in practice. The discussion in law school classrooms is intensely *legal*. Minnis (1994) says that the professor is generally indifferent 'to economic, social, or other contexts in which the events described in the judicial opinions might be viewed' (359). She points out that several scholars (e.g. Gopen 1984; White 1984) see close similarity between case analysis in the law classroom and the formalistic study of poetry: in both areas social, political, and cultural contexts are ignored in favor of an intense focus on language form, ambiguity, and possible meanings.

As we saw when we discussed the African-Americans' reading of the sentences from the Abigail and Gregory story, some people, in some of their social practices, connected often to their home and community-based Discourses, do not choose to isolate language from larger realms of experience. More generally, some families and social groups highly value cooperation, not competition, and some of these will not engage authority figures like parents or teachers, including law school teachers, in adversarial dialogue. (Minnis discusses the case of a Chicana law student in some detail, based on her own account, 382ff.) For some, being inducted into law school social practices means learning behaviors at odds with their other social practices that are constitutive of their other social identities. People *like me* don't do things *like that*; I'm not *that kind of person*. And yet law school summons me to do just that; to be precisely that kind of person.

The conflict, then, is not just that I am uncomfortable engaging in a new practice—much as a new physical activity might involve using new muscles. Rather, the conflict is between *who* I am summoned to be in this new Discourse (law school) and *who* I am in other Discourses that overtly conflict with—and sometimes have historically contested with—this new Discourse. Since Discourses (e.g. law school student and Hispanic-American of a certain sort) always exist and *mean* in juxtaposition to each other, performances in one often have meaning in regard to—and involve repercussions for—others. I can be asked in mind and body to 'mean against' some of my other social identities and their concomitant values.

Minnis recommends that, if they wish to treat their non-mainstream students fairly, law schools ought to 'make their assumptions, their values, the culture of the legal community—everything that comprises "thinking like a lawyer"—concrete and accessible' (385). While we agree with this advice, we also caution that making things concrete and accessible—rendering overt the 'rules of the game'—is not an educational panacea and in any case involves complex problems.

First, it cannot be done in any exhaustive manner. All that goes into thinking, acting, believing, valuing, dressing, interacting, reading, and writing *like a lawyer* cannot be put overtly in words. Whatever we could say, however long we took to say it, would be merely the tip of the iceberg. Furthermore, as overt knowledge it would not ground fluent behaviors any more than overt knowledge of dance steps can ground fluid dancing. In the absence of the full immersion that mainstream students are getting in the law school classroom, all that would happen with overt information is that non-mainstream students would engage in rather stilted performances that 'hypercorrected' what 'real' lawyers look, talk, and act like (Gee 1992; Perkins 1995).

This is certainly not to say that overt information could not help non-mainstream students know where to *focus* in the rich stream of texts and interactions that comprise law school. It is certainly not to recommend hiding aspects of language and interaction that lead to success and which we can describe and explicate. However, we simply cannot come close to describing and explicating even a small part of the 'game' in any realistic detail. The game works, in part, precisely because this cannot be done. Furthermore, no amount of description and explication will remove or necessarily mitigate the very real conflicts between Discourses.

Indeed, we need to know how better to exploit overt information within pedagogies of immersion and practice. But we cannot lose sight of the need to *change* the values, perspectives, and practices of Discourses like law school and the law, and not just render them more overt. And this leads us to our second point—such change is often very difficult to accomplish from *within* a Discourse.

The practices of a Discourse—like the practices of law school—contain in their forms of public interaction the 'mentalities' that learners are meant to internalize. Immersion in such practices—learning *inside* the procedures, rather than overly *about* them—ensures that a learner takes on perspectives, adopts a worldview, accepts a set of core values, and masters an identity without a great deal of critical and reflective awareness about these matters, or indeed about the Discourse itself.

No Discourse—not LA street gangs or LA police, not nuclear physicists, and certainly not new-capitalist businesses—wants to apprentice its newcomers to a process that makes them *question* its fundamental values and perspectives on the world. Such doubts and questions would not only undermine the Discourse, they would themselves undermine the sorts of fluent and fluid performances that mark one as a member of the Discourse in the first place.

Of course we, the authors of this book, believe that such critical reflection, such doubts and questions in regard to all limited perspectives are *good*. And all Discourses are by definition limited perspectives—limited in that they ignore or denigrate other Discourses' perspectives. Our point is, only, that few if any Discourses adopt this view in regard to their own (often tacit) core values, however much they gladly adopt it in regard to other Discourses.

This, indeed, is the great dilemma in regard to Discourses: it is difficult to criticize and change them either from *within* (they will simply dis-member us) or from *without* (why should they listen to an outsider?). And, in any case, what Discourse can stand above the others and dictate 'truth' and 'morality'? This dilemma is one that almost all work in sociocultural approaches to language and literacy runs into in some fashion or another. It becomes particularly acute when we fully engage with the Discourses of the new capitalism, as we will see in subsequent chapters.

In stating this problem, we are not offering a counsel of despair. Our point is rather that literacy and a sociocultural approach to it, are, in a sense, deeply *political* matters. We must take an overt values stance and engage in overt contest between Discourses, juxtaposing them and using one to change another. For all the very real challenges they face, bi-Discoursal people (people who have or are mastering two contesting or conflicting Discourses) are the ultimate sources of change, just as bilinguals very often are in the history of language. The non-mainstream law student who manages to bring off recognizable and acceptable law school Discourse practices, but infuses them with aspects of his or her other Discourses, is a source of challenge and change. So too are more overt challenges by those who have managed to get themselves—by hook or by crook—inside the door. So too are challenges from other Discourses, even from those who have never made it inside.

It is sometimes argued that such a Discourse perspective is 'deterministic', predestining people to success or failure in Discourses like law school on the basis of conflicts or resonances of their other Discourses with the new Discourse (Delpit 1995). Nothing could be further from the truth. The entire history of Discourses is a history of struggle, contestation, and change. Far from always losing, 'non-mainstream' people often win, and sometimes, for better or worse, they become a new 'mainstream', a new center of social power.

A Discourse perspective simply argues that historic sociocultural struggles are enacted by and on people's bodies and minds, often with much pain and injustice. These struggles are always between 'kinds' of people, but these 'kinds' are enacted by specific people with their specific and idiosyncratic bodies, minds, and feelings. This battle of 'kinds' acted out by specific individuals (who are actually many 'kinds' of people at once) causes some of the deepest perplexities in human life. The moral of a Discourse perspective is just this: no one, but no one, should feel like a 'loser' when they have lost a Discourse war (e.g. the non-mainstream law students whom Minnis discusses), given the subtle, complex, and often arbitrary ways in which Discourses connected to power stack the decks in favor of certain kinds of people.

III Goals and core values in the new work order

Our law school example is simply a paradigm case for us. You can substitute for 'law school' the label of many other Discourses, including current new-capitalist workplace Discourses and many new classroom Discourses (which we will see in Chapter 3), and most of our points remain the same. Learning works best—it is most enculturating, but (alas) also most indoctrinating—when it is done *inside* the social practices of a Discourse. Such 'deep' learning always involves the formation of new identities and thus possible conflicts with old ones. We will see in this book that new-capitalist businesses want such 'deep' learning, with its concomitant identity and value formations. These businesses are well aware, too, of the conflict among Discourses—for example, the conflict between traditional 'American individualism' and the 'teamwork' of the new work order, or the conflict between the traditional 'job' and the 'portfolio career' of the new capitalism. An elementary school student or a new worker at an electronics assembly plant are initiates into specific Discourses, Discourses that are fast changing under the forces of the new capitalism, just as much as any law school student is an initiate. We need theories of learning and knowledge that range equally over all such cases.   '

Learning—if it is not a senseless activity, which regrettably it sometimes is—is a process of entry into and participation in a Discourse. Unfortunately, a focus on children and schooling tends to obscure the role of social practices and Discourses. Some Discourses, like law, have a separate domain for (initial) initiation into the Discourse (namely law school). Others, including many Discourses connected to workplaces, do not engage in such a separation to any similar extent. In this case much learning and initiation into the Discourse occurs 'on the job'. In both cases, however, the connection between learning and participation in the 'mature' Discourse (law or work) is relatively clear. The same is true of family, community, and various public sphere Discourses.

School-based Discourses are quite anomalous in this respect. Schools don't merely separate learning from participation in 'mature' Discourses: they render the connection entirely mysterious. Schools and classrooms most certainly create Discourses; that is, they create social practices that integrate people, deeds, values, beliefs, words, tools, objects, and places. They create, as well, social positions (identities) for kinds of students and teachers. However, the Discourse of the school or classroom is primarily a Discourse devoted to learning—but, learning *for what*? Is it learning for participation in the school or classroom Discourse itself, or learning for Discourses outside school? Which Discourses outside school? And what sort of relationship to these outside Discourses should (or do) school and classroom Discourses contract?

We are not advocating easy answers here; rather we are pointing to complex questions and issues. The separation between school-based Discourses and outside Discourses may be a good thing, or it may not be. It all depends on how we answer such questions as 'What is the point (goal, purpose, vision) of school-based Discourses?' and 'What is the point (goal, purpose, vision) of this or that *specific* school-based Discourse (e.g., elementary school science or secondary school physics)?'.

The issue of *goals* is a particularly important one and will allow us to introduce one of the central concerns of this book: the changing nature of work in the new capitalism, a matter to which we have alluded several times. When we refer here to the new capitalism, we are specifically making reference to the thus far unevenly realized worldview contained in a large number of quasi-popular business texts. Typical and well-known examples from a seemingly inexhaustible supply are: Bennis, Parikh & Lessem 1994; Boyett and Conn 1992; Champy 1995; Crosby 1994; Cross, Feather & Lynch 1994; Davidow & Malone 1992; Dobyns & Crawford-Mason 1991; Drucker 1993; Hamel & Prahalad 1994; Hammer & Champy 1993; Handy 1989, 1994; Imparato & Harari 1994; Lipnack & Stamps 1993; Peters 1992, 1994; Sashkin & Kiser 1993; Senge 1991. The worldview is also regularly represented in any popular business magazine (e.g. *Fortune*). We will see in this book that the new work order emerging in the new capitalism allows us to refocus a number of issues crucial to sociocultural approaches to literacy and learning. One of these is the issue of goals—the 'point' of why we do what we do.

While we discuss the new capitalism at length in the next chapter, here we want to take up a major change in many work-based Discourses, a change in the 'kinds' of workers that are summoned forth and positioned within these Discourses. We pointed out above that Discourses are essentially about the social (and historical) construction of 'kinds' of people (e.g. scientific psychologists or street gang members). While this may seem a fancy theoretical notion—and indeed we have been influenced here by the work of the philosopher Ian Hacking (1986, 1994)—it is a notion readily appealed to in literature written by new-capitalist business people and consultants. For example, consider James Champy—a co-inventor of reengineering, a popular new-capitalist business reform—on the differences between how hiring was done under the rubric of the old capitalism and how it will be done in the new:

Let me put the difference between hiring processes then and now in the most chilling way I can think of. Today, *its not only what you know that counts, it's what kind of person you are* [italics in text]. What kind of person you are means, essentially, whether you'll be able to live up to, or at least aspire to, the 'values' both social and work-related that I listed . . . (Champy 1995: 157).

The values that Champy refers to are his version of the values of the new capitalism, which we will discuss in a moment. The changes in the kinds of people that capitalist workplaces wish to construct have major implications for the nature of schools and schooling, as well as for society as a whole. The issue of goals, as we will now see, is one way to begin to get at these implications.

From the end of World War II until the early 1970s the 'old' industrial mass-market capitalism, especially in the United States, had massive and unsaturated markets for consumer goods (Leach 1993). This led to unprecedented economic success for large corporations marketing mass-produced goods. By today's standards, competition was not particularly stiff: much of it was within the borders of nation states over which these large corporations exercised a great deal of control. What was global was carried out in the context of US economic and political hegemony.

This economic climate produced two large categories of workers. The first category was made up of low-level workers hired 'from the neck down' to engage in allegedly mindless, repetitive, and meaningless pieces of tasks, the wholes of which they did not need to understand and certainly had no control over. The auto worker on the assembly line became a symbol of this sort of worker.

The second category was made up of 'middle managers' who existed in large, bureaucratic, and heavily hierarchical corporations to pass information between the top and the bottom of the hierarchy and to supervise bottom-line workers. These middle managers (trained in business schools for the most part) were allegedly the professional 'brains' of the corporation, those who supposedly understood and supervised its work systems.

The new capitalism has much less interest in either of these kinds of workers. Today, markets in the developed world are saturated with consumer goods, and have been for some time. Furthermore, competition is now truly global (Barnet & Cavanagh 1994). And customers, with more sophistication and information, and more choices, than ever before, are fickle. Finally, changes in technology and information systems have immensely increased the pace of change and the ability of smaller organizations to compete against larger, more tradition-bound outfits. All these trends have led to hypercompetition.

The remaining backwaters of the old capitalism apart, in this hypercompetitive, science-and-technology-driven, fast-paced world only businesses that produce the highest quality for the best price to just the right niche market can survive and flourish. Or at least that is the ideology of the theories and practices driving workplace changes across the developed world.

In this sort of capitalism, 'commodities'—which drove the old capitalism—are problematic. By the time a product or service has become a commodity, it has become rather standardized, 'normal', a taken-for-granted item available to large numbers of people. This means that lots of companies will be producing it with more and more pressure on prices and markets.

The successful company in an age of cut-throat competition and constant change must keep innovating products and services perfectly dovetailed to the lifestyle and identity of a particular group of people or to the specific needs of another company. Better yet, these products and services ought to be customized for each customer (person or company), something that new computer-driven technologies readily allow in many cases. Only in this way can a business 'own' its customers. New-capitalist businesses must even create new kinds of customers (note, 'kinds of people' again) so as to create new niches.

However, even if it is successful, a business will not own its 'kinds of customers' long without constantly varying and improving its products or services and innovating new ones. Otherwise, fickle customers will change their allegiances in the sea of competition running after their money and their identities.

The new capitalism, because of these changes, wants and needs far fewer managers in the middle between the top and bottom of a business. Middle managers, as they pass information back and forth, slow the business down just when it should be responding as rapidly as possible to its customers. They insulate it from the fast-changing market at a time when businesses must respond quickly and adaptively. They bloat large companies just when they must get as 'lean and mean' as possible. They separate leaders from workers who are on the front-line closest to the customers and who most deeply affect their level of satisfaction.

If the ranks of the middle mangers are to be seriously thinned, much of their knowledge, information, and responsibility must be pushed down to the lower-level workers. In fact, it is a principle of the new capitalism to push down control and responsibility to the lowest possible level, closest to the actual products, services, and customers of the business. This, however, requires workers now who can learn and adapt quickly, think for themselves, take responsibility, make decisions, and communicate what they need and know to leaders who coach, supply, and inspire them.

Workers must now take responsibility, usually in teams, for whole and meaningful tasks which they understand and seek to improve. Furthermore, they must interface with technical information (e.g. statistical quality control devices) and sophisticated technologies (e.g. computers, telecommunications, robots). Gone then—except, again, in the backwaters of the old capitalism—are workers hired from the neck down and simply told what to do.

Thus far we have canvassed an 'ideology', a vision of a world in the making. The 'real' world is, of course, much more complex. We take up concrete examples of the interaction of this ideology and the real world in Chapters 4, 5, and 6. In Chapter 2 we offer a more refined statement of 'visions' of the new capitalism and a more substantive critique. Here we are after the way in which goals and values emerge from the logic of this ideology and the practices to which it gives rise.

The changes we have surveyed above offer the new capitalism its greatest challenge: how to gain the full loyalty and trust of newly empowered workers so that they will throw themselves heart and soul into the work of the company in very risky times. In a hypercompetitive, fast-changing environment workers must be 'eager to stay', but also 'ready to leave' if the business is failing or even if it must innovate new projects that no longer require the core competencies of the current workers. This is a hard situation, indeed, within which to motivate people.

Leaders can scarcely achieve this motivation by trying to assert top-down control over their newly empowered workers. Newly *empowered* workers won't tolerate being ordered around and, in any case, it is not motivating. However, they can hardly be allowed to work (act, believe, and value) against the interests of the business, its leaders, and its shareholders. What, then, ensures trust, loyalty, and full 'over the top' commitment?

In facing this challenge the new capitalism puts a great deal of faith in creating goals, core values, a vision, a 'culture'—whatever one wishes to call it (*we* would call it creating a Discourse)—and communicating it to workers (partners). To get a feeling for how this works, let's listen at some length to Champy again about what it takes for a business to mobilize for 'the total struggle that today's chaotic markets and customer-driven competition demands' (Champy 1995: 40):

> It takes leadership, of course, but a leadership of a new kind. I mean the capacity to articulate the reasons—the *motivating explanations*—why this business and its people must do what they're being called on to do . . . (40).

> People work for a paycheck, sure. But if that's the only reason they can find for going to work every day, they won't work with the imagination, the resourcefulness, the steady willingness, and the sensitivity to the marketplace that we've got to promote all the way through the organization if we want to prevail in today's environment (41).

> The fact is that with authority now being redistributed throughout the organization, there is no *the* leader. Everyone must be a leader; everyone, that is to say, must answer questions about the business's purpose—and ask questions, too (41).

> Mobilization for today must be total mobilization, up, down, and sideways. This means that everyone must be 'in the know.' Unless they are, you can forget about getting a total mobilization; in fact, everyone *not* in the know will see nothing in your efforts but a conspiracy. No one is going to go through the ordeal of total mobilization for change without knowing why, or what for (47).

> That manager may not be able to provide soothing words, but he or she can provide the next best thing—reasons and a picture of the future. Everyone wants reasons and that picture, and in the reengineering effort everyone had better have them (48).

> A manager's statement of purpose and vision is important in this task of *signification*. It's the master script, if you will, in which we all play out our different roles. It's the corporate meaning in which we find our personal meaning (58).

The ideology of the new capitalism claims that the goal, vision, or purpose of a successful business cannot merely be profit. This simply won't motivate all workers/partners to commit themselves fully in a hypercompetitive world requiring 'over the top' effort. Thus these new businesses seek to create core values that underlie, integrate, and guide the social practices of their distinctive Discourses.

In fact, we can put the matter this way: new capitalist businesses seek quite overtly to create and sustain Discourses with their distinctive social identities tied to distinctive ways of thinking, interacting, valuing, and so forth. Of course, workplaces have always constituted Discourses; it is just that the new capitalism is now quite open about the need to *socialize* people into 'communities of practice' that position people to be certain kinds of people. They now realize that they are in the business of creating and sustaining Discourses, though they don't use this term.

As an example of the nature of 'beyond profit' core values, consider those espoused by three well-known companies—the sorts of things that ground the 'reasons why we are here', the 'reasons' that leaders are to communicate to everyone in the business (the lists set out below are adapted from Collins & Porras 1994: 68–69). These core values are specific expressions within specific companies of the more general version of new-capitalist values that Champy celebrates in his call for new kinds of persons at work.

Johnson & Johnson (a pharmaceutical company)
- The company exists 'to alleviate pain and disease'
- 'We have a hierarchy of responsibilities: customers first, employees second, society at large third, and shareholders fourth'
- Individual opportunity and reward based on merit
- Decentralization = Creativity = Productivity

Philip Morris (cigarettes and many other products)
- The right to personal freedom of choice (to smoke, to buy whatever one wants) is worth defending
- Winning—being the best and beating others
- Encouraging individual initiative
- Opportunity to achieve based on merit, not gender, race, or class
- Hard work and continuous self-improvement

Walt Disney (entertainment)
- No cynicism allowed
- Fanatical attention to consistency and detail
- Continuous progress via creativity, dreams, and imagination
- Fanatical control and preservation of Disney's 'magic' image
- 'To bring happiness to millions' and to celebrate, nurture, and promulgate 'wholesome American values'

Note that the core values of these three companies create quite different 'moral universes' (notice, too, how selling cigarettes managed to get within a wider and more uplifting set of values). Even if we consider just this aspect of the new capitalism—its urge to create the value-outlines of its new Discourses quite overtly—we see several crucial issues for a sociocultural approach to learning and literacy.

First: In the case of any Discourse we can make a distinction between espoused goals and values and the goals and values that actually emerge in practice. These are not always, not even usually, in complete agreement with each other in any Discourse. Very often there is tension and even contradiction between them. The distinction here is similar to the distinction that has often been made in the case of schooling between the 'overt curriculum' and the 'hidden curriculum'.

New-capitalist businesses claim strongly that they wish to align their overt values and their actual practices. They are very much devoted to bringing the espoused goals and visions of their Discourse into line with the actual social practices of their partners, where 'partners' is supposed to include managers and leaders as well as front-line workers.

They attempt this alignment by overt 'sociotechnical engineering' of their social practices and ultimately of their partners. How much we should trust the rhetoric of the new capitalism, in its more humane aspects, is a matter we take up in subsequent chapters. However, we believe that one of the main motifs of our new world will be the attempt by the new capitalism to create new kinds of people by changing not just their overt viewpoints but their actual practices: to 'reengineer' people in its image.

Second: In its attempts to create new kinds of workers/partners, the new capitalism will put pressure on other learning-centered Discourses to help produce such kinds of people. In particular, the new capitalism will progressively recruit schools to produce suitable 'subjects' or 'citizens' for new-capitalist Discourse in general and its manifestations in specific Discourses (those implied, for example, by the specific core values listed above for three companies). It will do this, much as law school produces suitable 'citizens' for the Discourse of law. This pressure is very much under way as we speak and is dealt with at greater length in Chapter 3.

Third: As new-capitalist businesses get overt about their (supposed) goals and visions, we need a renewed discussion of the goals of schools and schooling, as well as the goals of 'lifelong learning'. What should the relationship between school and work be? How should schools engage with the new capitalism? What should our engagement as critical theorists be? Are schools really where the 'action' is in regard to social justice and equity? What, for instance, is the role of the school in social melioration when business claims to be no longer solely about profit, but also about social visions of empowered lifelong learners? How should we construe learning and knowledge in general in a world where the new capitalism progressively seeks to define what counts as learning and knowledge in a 'knowledge economy' made up of 'knowledge workers' doing 'knowledge work'? These questions, too, we believe, will be major motifs in our new world.

Fourth: Are new-capitalist attempts to define and 'construct' new kinds of empowered, fulfilled, committed, and intelligent workers merely high-tech/high-touch forms of mind control—a new soft-touch hegemony—or are they a more humane face of capitalism? What is the role of the 'critical' part of sociocultural studies in such a world—will critique, as critical theory defines it, help or cripple workers in the new capitalism? (Recall Disney's 'no cynicism'.) How can we ensure that we do not use workers' and students' allegiance to *our* politics as a sign of their liberation (or should we?), while still helping to ensure that they are not dupes of the new capitalism? Are we sociocultural theorists an endangered species in a world where the center of gravity of what counts as learning and knowledge, as well as 'citizenship', is switching from schools to globalized workplaces and networks? Here, too, we argue, are major themes for the new world. The following chapters deal with many of these themes: not to give definitive answers, but rather to encourage all concerned to construct their own theories and their own critiques in order to better engage in reflective practice in our 'new times'.

2   Fast capitalism: theory and practice

It's old news that, during the past twenty years or so, the realm of work has changed dramatically across the developed world as part of a profound global economic restructuring. It is important, however, to ask how much of the new capitalism and its attendant new work order is already a reality and how much of it is as yet only on paper. Of course, the 'real world' is a more complex place than either the research literature or popular books usually allow, notwithstanding the fact that the textual world of the new capitalism is a multiple one. There are in fact a good many forms of new-capitalist literature: scholarly research, postmodern critiques, government policy documents, business books and popular accounts.

One form of literature that we are particularly concerned with in this chapter may be called 'fast capitalist texts'. These texts, produced mainly by business managers and consultants, seek to attend as textual midwives at the birth of the new work order: books such as Joseph Boyett and Henry Conn's *Workplace 2000* (1992), Tom Peters' *Liberation Management* (1992), Peter Senge's *The Fifth Discipline* (1991), and Hammer & Champy's *Reengineering the Corporation* (1993), and many more (see references in Section III of Chapter 1). Such books tell what has quickly become the 'mainline' popular story about the social, work, and economic changes of our new times.

Fast capitalist texts create on paper a version of the new work order that their authors are trying hard to enact in the world. In this chapter we address the fast capitalist version of the world as a specific, ideologically loaded 'story'—but a story that may very well become true, especially in the absence of competing and equally powerful alternative stories. We also address the 'absences' and 'silences' in fast capitalist texts, areas in which these texts gloss over the complexities

24

of the real world. (Later chapters (especially 4, 5, and 6) deal more specifically with the real world and its attendant tensions with the fast capitalist world on paper.)

At the same time, the 'world on paper' is important: how we think and write about the world has a great deal to do with how we act in it and, thus, what it becomes in reality.

Fast capitalist texts are a mixed genre: a mix of history and description, prophecy, warning, proscriptions and recommendations, parables (stories of success and failure), and large doses of utopianism. They announce a new 'enchanted workplace', where hierarchy is dead and partners engage in meaningful but often fast-paced and stressful work in a collaborative environment of mutual commitment and trust.

At various points below we juxtapose these celebratory and hortatory fast capitalist texts with accounts provided in the more formal research-based scholarly literature (e.g. Best 1990; Block 1990; Carnoy *et al.* 1993; Thurow 1992; see Levett & Lankshear 1994 for an overview). Even here there is no one true story to be had, only reasoned debate melded with compassion and a concern for morality and social justice, the latter all too often missing from fast capitalist texts.

We have not, however, come simply to dismiss fast capitalist texts, but rather to engage with them. They are a partial window on a fast-changing world. The worldview of our fast capitalist texts has massive implications for schools, workplace learning, and the role of the university in society—issues we take up in the following chapter. In the end, however, we believe we must squarely face the moral shortcomings of both fast capitalist texts and the new work order they have already helped to partly usher in.

I The fast capitalist story

Fast capitalist texts have been very influential in their short life to date. They are important not only in the domains of business and work—their vision and values have deeply informed contemporary calls for reform both in adult education and training and in schools across the developed world (see next chapter). And they are changing the ways in which people think about relationships among business, education, government, and society at large.

The fast capitalist storyline that we offer here is, of course, derived from many texts. Being a general account, it is not entirely fair to some of the particularities and nuances in specific fast capitalist texts. Nonetheless, we believe it is a fair representation of what emerges from that literature as a whole.

What we are really talking about here is a textual creation of a new Discourse (Gee 1996) with new social identities: new bosses (now 'coaches' and 'leaders'), new middle managers (now 'team leaders'), new workers (now 'associates', 'partners', 'knowledge workers'), and new customers (now also 'partners' and 'insiders', who are said to drive the whole process). The issues are deeper still: the fast capitalist version of the new capitalism is, as we will see, profoundly imperialistic, seeking to take over practices and social identities that are (or were) the terrain of other Discourses connected to churches, communities, universities, and governments.

So, here's the basic fast capitalist story, one that is now so often repeated that it rolls rather effortlessly off the tongue or the keyboard (Gee 1994; Gee & Lankshear 1995).

The very structure and needs of a new and transformed capitalism (sometimes called 'post-capitalism', e.g. Drucker 1993) is leading, it is said, to a more meaningful, humane, and socially just—though more stressful—workplace. The old capitalism was based on the mass pro-duction of (relatively uniform) goods by large, hierarchically structured corporations serving a commodities-starved, but progressively richer post–World War II population in the developed world. Workers, hired from the neck down had only to follow directions and mechanically carry out a rather meaningless piece of a process they did not need to understand as a whole, and certainly did not control (this is the heart of so-called Fordism).

The new capitalism is based on the design, production, and mar-keting of 'high quality' goods and services for now saturated markets. In the developed world today, economic survival is contingent on selling newer and ever more perfect(ed) customized (individualized) goods and services to niche markets—that is, to groups of people who come to define and change their identities by the sorts of goods and services they consume. The emphasis now is on the (active) knowledge and flexible learning needed to design, market, perfect, and vary goods and services as symbols of identity, not on the actual product itself as a material good. And, thanks to technological and social changes, this sort of 'quality' competition is now fully globalized. The winners design customized products and services on time/on demand faster and more perfectly than their global competition does or they go out of business.

The new capitalism is driven—according to our fast capitalist texts—by such factors as greatly increased global hypercompetition, massive technological changes, and the demands and desires of increasingly sophisticated consumers (we return below to this latter factor). These factors force everyone to compete on the basis of ever more perfected and customized products and services for ever more discriminating and knowledgeable customers. Once you imagine everyone competing on this basis, however, a tension emerges. As one company 'perfects' its product, the only basis on which another company can outcompete it is to make a yet more perfect product, one more closely designed to the customer's needs, interests, and desires, more quickly delivered to the market, and more swiftly changed and perfected yet again so as to create new desires and customers. The end result is the creation of the most 'lean and mean', quick and efficient, customer-pleasing and customer-creating businesses possible. Ever more creative and perfect products and services are created and re-created at ever faster rates.

To give a sense of the rather paradoxical way in which these things are talked about, let us develop a pastiche from the bestselling book, *Reengineering the Corporation* (Hammer & Champy 1993: 11, 17, 18–24).

> Advanced technologies, the disappearance of boundaries between national markets, and the altered expectations of customers who now have more choices than ever before have combined to make the goals, methods, and basic organizing principles of the classical American corporation sadly obsolete. . . .
>
> Three forces, separately and in combination, are driving today's companies deeper and deeper into territory that most of their executives and managers find frighteningly unfamiliar. We call these forces the three Cs: Customers, Competition, and Change. . . .
>
> . . .The mass market has broken into pieces, some as small as a single customer. Individual customers—whether consumers or industrial firms—demand that they be treated individually. . . .
>
> . . . It used to be so simple: The company that could get to market with an acceptable product or service at the best price would get a sale. Now, not only does more competition exist, it's of many different kinds. Good performers drive out the inferior, because the lowest price, the highest quality, the best service available from any one of them soon becomes the standard for all competitors. Adequate is no longer good enough.
>
> . . . change has become both pervasive and persistent. It *is* normality. Moreover, the pace of change has accelerated. With

globalization of the economy, companies face a greater number of competitors, each one of which may introduce product and service innovations to the market. The rapidity of technological change also promotes innovation. Product life cycles have gone from years to months.

'Perfection' becomes 'standard'; 'change' becomes 'normality'. In these texts words take on new meanings. This sort of language has become so worn and smooth in such a short time that we almost miss the paradox. To relieve the sense of paradox it seems that one must believe that there are no substantive constraints on the production of new ideas, new desires, new customers, new products and services— a faith that must, we would think, go hand in hand with a belief that modern science and technology render 'finite' resources 'infinitely expandable' on the basis of ever new technologies and new solutions to social and economic problems. In fact, we will see that a belief in the powers of science and technology is one of the core utopian aspects of fast capitalist texts.

'Customization' is a watchword here: economic changes—largely due to the globalization and intensification of competition, demand, and science and technology—allow businesses to personalize their products and services to the identities of specific groups of people, even to individuals. In fact, as we have already observed, these economic changes and technological changes demand and allow the creation and transformation of identities. A new product or service must be first to the market, create or capture a niche, be progressively varied and perfected so as to 'own' that niche, and eventually be transformed into (or deserted for) a new product or service when fierce global competition eventually renders the product or service a cheap and humdrum 'commodity'. That is, the new capitalism is not about commodities, then, as was the old. To survive, businesses must sell products and services that are too new and too customized to particular identities to be mere commodities. Commodities are the residue of each new fast capitalist success story.

This is where 'knowledge' comes in: what is important is not the material product or the brute service, rather it is the knowledge it takes to innovate, design, efficiently produce, market, and transform products and services as symbols of identity and lifestyle in a high risk world. When we hear, as we often do, terms like 'knowledge work' and 'knowledge society', we should be well aware that knowledge is being talked about in the framework we have just summarized. Given the honorific connotations of the word 'knowledge', it would be best, perhaps, to have another word here. But as we will see below, part of the way in which fast capitalist texts 'grab us' is that they use words that name things which nearly all of us like but which, on reflection are seen to mean slightly (and sometimes *very*) different things in fast capitalist texts than they might mean to many of us: words like 'liberation', 'empowerment', 'trust', 'vision', 'collaboration', 'teams', 'self-directed learning', 'quality', and many more.

The logic of fast capitalist competition carries the implication that a good many changes must occur in organizational structures and ultimately in society as a whole. Only those businesses that are lean and mean i.e., have no non-value-adding people and close to the customer (i.e. local and personal in effect, even if huge and global in reality) will succeed. One result is that the large, hierarchically struc- tured, depersonalized corporations of the old capitalism must be broken into smaller, more personal and locally flavored workplaces in which hierarchy is greatly reduced (we get so-called 'flat hierarchies'). The middle managers of old-style corporations disappear or take on new roles (either adding value directly by front-line work or serving as team leaders).

We should be clear here, though: very often the 'localism' and 'smallness' of the new capitalism are a false impression. The business we deal with is, in reality, a global megacorporation but the manifes- tation of it we face takes on all the coloring of a small, local, self-contained outfit (see Tom Peters' remarks about 'mom and pop' businesses below). Furthermore, local coloring is often as much a creation by the business of a new identity (e.g. a 'Chinese checking account' reflecting the bank's needs and desires about such matters, not substantive aspects of any traditional Chinese culture apart from lan- guage), as it is an 'authentic' expression of a local community.

As noted earlier, middle management (the core creation of the old capitalism and its attendant business schools; see Kotter 1995) had previously existed to supervise the workers and to pass information up and down the hierarchy between the (insulated) bosses and the workers; additionally, middle managers were the ones who were supposed to understand the processes and systems of the workplace. The logic of the new work order is that the roles and responsibilities of the middle will pass to the front-line workers themselves (formerly, the bottom of the hierarchy). Workers will be transformed into committed 'partners' who engage in meaningful work, fully understand and control their jobs, supervise themselves, and actively seek to improve their perfor- mance through communicating clearly their knowledge and needs.

Such 'motivated' workers can no longer be 'ordered' around by 'bosses'. As partners, they can only be 'developed', 'coached', and 'supported'. Hierarchy is gone, egalitarianism is in. Workers increasingly assume managerial roles in settings where work centers on collaborative (team-based) 'projects'. Concomitantly, they must take responsibility for their own careers, and not leave such responsibility to businesses or governments. When a project is over (perfected), they must be willing to move on to develop their own 'portfolio' of skills and achievements. They must not expect a business to sustain them in the long run, a business that may need, as it develops new products and services, to hire new teams for new projects. It is not uncommon to find in fast capitalist literature something analogous to making a movie for a studio. The team works together until the movie is finished and then leaves the studio. Tom Peters addresses these themes in his characteristic manner thus:

> The message [to chiefs] is clear: (1) trust, (2) 'they' can handle 'it' (whatever 'it' is), (3) you're only in control when you're out of control ('head' of a flat, radically decentralized 'organization') (Peters 1992: 758–59).

> Another big step, it turns out: the entrepreneurizing of every job. One hundred percent of employees turned into 'business people' is, I contend, no pipe dream. With a bit of imagination (okay, more than a bit), the average job—actually, every job—can become an entrepreneurial challenge. Letting go means letting the person alone to experience those Maalox moments—that is, true, genuine, no-baloney ownership in the gut. If there's no deep-seated, psychological ownership, there's no ownership. Period (Peters 1994: 67, 72, 80–81).

Since workers (now 'partners') will now find meaning in their jobs and will personally buy the 'vision' of the company, they should no longer need supervision, and should be willing both to work harder for longer hours and to share in the risks and potential losses (and profits) of the company. There is also a greater emphasis on workers working in teams collaboratively, since such teams can be more efficient than any single member, if they operate correctly. And furthermore teams ensure that workers can supervise each other, given that individual members of a team are rewarded or penalized on the basis of the team's performance, not just their own.

Communication is all-important in this world, as the workers tell the bosses (now the leaders or coaches) what they need in order to do their jobs optimally, and share with the leaders what they know about their jobs and how to improve performance and quality. And thus the workers take over themselves some of the former roles of the missing middle managers. In their turn, the leaders communicate a vision (higher order values and goals) to their worker/partners. Of course, some middle managers remain, but they become 'consultants', 'project directors', 'team leaders', 'knowledge brokers', 'facilitators', 'mediators', or 'assistant coaches'.

II A dilemma in the new work order

From the above discussion it should be apparent that the new work order faces some profound dilemmas. For example, in a lean and mean organization with no non-value-adding partners (i.e. no one around just to ensure that someone else does his or her job), the full 'over the top' commitment and loyalty of each worker to the team, to the project, and to the organization is absolutely crucial. Otherwise, in a fiercely competitive world, an organization with still more committed employees will win out. But how does one get such commitment?

Workers trained in the old capitalism may have a very hard time adapting or changing their values and their attitudes toward work and workplaces. In fact, there is a danger of widespread cynicism in the workforce, based on the idea that fast capitalist practices are meant to 'dupe' the worker into working harder and longer for less reward—or at least with greater risk—in the service of elites who still formulate the basic vision in their own interests. Thus we see, in fast capitalist texts, a strong emphasis on bringing about change in schools and thereby changing the values and attitudes of tomorrow's workers.

Fast capitalist texts center on two competing solutions to the problem of how to get full commitment. One solution is 'visionary leadership'. In fact, some texts almost make a fetish of vision and charismatic leadership:

> *Workplace 2000* leaders will have a vision of the future . . . Well, it
> isn't 'build market share' and certainly not 'make money.' A vision
> is much broader and more compelling. It's a dream and an ideal.
> It's nothing less than 'changing the world.' The leader visualizes an
> ultimate purpose or mission for the organization that is so
> inspirational followers will voluntarily suspend rational judgment
> about the probability of success . . . Leaders visualize a larger
> reality and transmit that vision to others (Boyett & Conn 1992: 147).

Such leadership is held to be a (or *the*) chief motivational tool for 'Workplace 2000':

> . . . people feel empowered when they feel confident and in control. Leaders empower people. And empowerment is an emotional and motivational high. No task seems too difficult. No outcome seems too impossible or, at least, unworthy of valiant effort. The leader's efforts at empowerment are varied, but all aimed at the same outcome—followers who have ever increasing faith in their own abilities (ibid: 156–57).

This fast capitalist stress on vision (stemming from charismatic business leaders) is the leading edge of imperialism. Since businesses can no longer be solely about profit, it is said, they are now in competition with churches, governments, and universities in the framing and conduct of social and moral agendas. In fact, many fast capitalist texts are quite sceptical about how much the cause of 'social amelioration' has been advanced by non-business institutions like governments, churches, and universities—while businesses successfully gained profits in the old capitalism. They appear to believe it is time to center social and futuristic visions of society in the business world.

There are people who ask: Can businesses really expect that newly empowered workers will 'irrationally' follow the lead of a visionary? How many businesses can rely on getting and keeping such a charismatic leader in any case? Whence we come to the second proffered solution to gaining 'over the top' commitment: not visionary leaders but the creation and maintenance in the organization of 'core values' and a culture that induces (socializes) everyone into such values:

> A charismatic visionary leader is absolutely *not required* for a visionary company and, in fact, can be detrimental to a company's long-term prospects. [Successful companies] seek profits, but they're equally guided by a core ideology—core values and sense of purpose beyond just making money. There is no 'right' set of core values for being a visionary company. Core values in a visionary company don't even have to be 'enlightened' or 'humanistic,' although they often are. The crucial variable is not the content of a company's ideology, but how deeply it *believes* its ideology and how consistently it lives, breathes, and expresses it in all that it does (Collins & Porras 1994: 8).

We discussed the issue of culture and core values in Chapter 1 (where you can find specific examples of the core values of some highly successful corporations). Of course, talk of core values and the creation of cultures is as imperialistic as talk of visionary leadership:

in both cases we get businesses as the site of values beyond profit, values that traditionally have been centered in non-business institutions.

The imperialism of the fast capitalist Discourse goes deeper still. Fast capitalist texts are not simply attempts to describe a reality already in place; they are what we might call 'projective' or 'enactive' texts (Gee 1994). Written by business leaders and consultants to business, they are almost always parts of larger projects to enact (to call into being) a vision of a new world. Their vision of new values, new social purposes and practices, and new social identities is strikingly totalizing. Just as new identities are being formed (worker as partner; boss as coach and designer of others' learning processes), so, too, old divisions, such as that between 'public' and 'private', are being effaced. Boyett and Conn capture this neatly. They refer to David Kirp and Douglas Rice's observation that 'What these 'work hard, play hard' companies want is nothing less than total responsibility and over-the-edge loyalty . . . Employees are constantly on view and the line between work and play, the line between public and private becomes fuzzy . . .' (Boyett & Conn 1992: 40; see also Kirp & Rice 1988: 79). Boyett and Conn comment further as follows:

> Even social gatherings in *Workplace 2000* will take on special meanings. Here's how journalist Robert Howard, author of Brave New *Workplace*, described the kind of company-sponsored social occasion we will see more of in the future: '[E]ven the archetypal beer bust . . . is not some trivial social occasion (or, as one manager says, 'not just everyone sitting around drinking beer'). It is a ritual of corporate loyalty and belonging. The purpose of such rituals, says our manager, 'is to have everyone know where things are going, from the top level people all the way to little Suzy down there stuffing the printed circuit board. She gets information on what the product is for. She has an idea of the whole board'. . .
>
> Through this broad-based structure of motivation, she is 'locked in mentally' to the future of the company. It is a kind of parallel production process whose purpose is to manufacture not products, but attitudes and expectations (Boyett & Conn 1992: 40; see also Howard 1984: 257).

The public and private divide is not simply erased by the leakage of work practices and values into other spheres of life. Many new-capitalist books blur the divide between organizations and private lives: the way in which one should run an organization or one's work is also the way in which one should run one's personal life. For example, just as 'quality' at work means 'doing a *complete* job' with no detail left undone and no defect uncovered, so, too, leading one's personal life means achieving similar 'completeness' in one's life as a whole (Crosby

1994). Or, just as a business must make a clear distinction between its core (where it devotes most of its resources and efforts) and its periphery (which it recruits only as needed and dispenses with afterwards), each of us should devote the main resources of our lives to our core mission based on our core competencies and offload everything else to others (Handy 1994).

Or, to take another example, just as a business requires visionary leadership that has a vision of the future, our lives require such a vision to motivate us beyond our mundane daily struggle for existence (Bennis, Parikh and Lessem 1994). Or, a final example, just as a new-capitalist business is a set of projects adapted to a fast-changing world, held together by a set of core values, not by any predicable set of products or services, so, too, our lives turn out to be a portfolio of projects (some for money, some not for money), not one linear progression along a single line (Handy 1994).

The point here is that, while these are all rather prosaic suggestions, they are in fact extensions, to the sphere of everyday life, of detailed 'business proposals', formulated by business consultants. Fast capitalist texts often take on the flavor of a new business-and-market-linked existentialism. It is here that fast capitalism comes closest to colonizing the 'lifeworld' (Habermas 1984)—that domain in which each of us is a (culturally specific) normal, unspecialized person.

The management rhetoric and ideology of fast capitalism, centered on the newly 'enchanted', (because 'meaningful'), workplace is, however, 'easily vulnerable to abuses of power and [to] the elaborate manipulation of people and values':

> The promise of the enchanted workplace is a promise of meaning, with the corporation as the mediator between work and the self. In order to cash in on the meanings of the enchanted workplace, however, the workers must cleave to a set of ends—'superordinate goals', 'corporate culture', whatever—that 'like the basic postulates of a mathematical system', is posited in advance. Workers rarely have the opportunity to influence the content of those ends, let alone play an active role in their formation . . . As a result, the necessity of allegiance to a set of ends over which one has little control can become a recipe for a dangerous corporate intrusiveness that produces not autonomy and freedom, but enforced conformity, not genuine participation, but a kind of high-touch coercion (Boyett & Conn 1992: 114–15, quoting Howard 1984: 262).

We have seen that, for the resolution of this dilemma, fast capitalist texts point to having trust in workers/partners and allowing them to have 'real control' over their work. However, fast capitalist texts rarely contain any notion of empowering employees to assess and (re)frame the *goals* of the organization or to generate a more powerful *role* for themselves in decision-making processes dealing with such matters as, say, job tenure or whether or not to 'downsize' or 'go offshore'. Furthermore, while fast capitalism requires total commitment on the part of workers/partners, this commitment is not necessarily reciprocated in many of the ways that might seem necessary for engendering that commitment in the first place. An excerpt from the *Boston Globe* puts this point in perspective:

> For those lucky enough to snag a job, permanence is a thing of the past. 'For the corporation I work with, at one point in time they would talk about how "We promise our workers lifetime employment," says James Medoff, a Harvard economics professor. 'Now they say with a big smile, "We want you to be eager to stay, but ready to leave".' (*Boston Sunday Globe* 16 October 1994, 'Students facing difficult job search', by Barbara Carton)

It is worth noting here that states of being such as 'being eager to stay but ready to go' are not especially common. They appear, in fact, to be internally contradictory. To be sure, they require a very specific construal of identity: an asocial independent entrepreneur contracting out her or his own work who must, ironically, be strongly collaborative when on the job. Of course, it is the 'need' for such new identities that requires the creation of a new Discourse in the first place.

For now, we can sum up in this way: the new capitalism is fundamentally about *privatization*. By this we mean that it advocates that, by and large, everything—business, social processes, private lives—ought to be *unregulated* except by the forces of competition ('markets') defined around *quality* as determined by 'customers' (where our family and friends are, in our private lives, our 'customers'). *Customization* is, in the sphere of design and production, a form of privatization. Privatization throws all of us—and is meant to—on our own resources, or on resources of our (perhaps temporary) 'team' or 'tribe', demanding that we take responsibility for our own lives, which themselves are seen now as like businesses (competing in various 'markets').

III Silences in fast capitalist texts

We will discuss salient 'silences' in fast capitalist texts by considering several fundamental features of the new world economy as identified by Manuel Castells (1993). We will be discussing dysutopian aspects of the emerging new-capitalist world, aspects that go virtually unmentioned in fast capitalist texts.

1. The first feature is that the bases of productivity in the new capitalism depend increasingly on applying science and technology in processes of production, distribution, consumption, and change. Increased productivity is no longer mainly a matter of just injecting more labor and/or capital into the production process. Instead, the edge in productivity is generated by 'new inputs' consisting of 'the deeper penetration of science, technology, labor skills, and management know-how' (Castells 1993: 15–16).

What do our fast capitalist texts have to say about this? One would gain little feeling for the debates and dilemmas surrounding science and technology in the new capitalism simply from reading fast capitalist texts. Much of the fast capitalist literature, in fact, treats science and technology as the basis for a new utopia. It is deeply silent about the dysfunctional side of scientific and technological changes.

Joe Bailey (1988) has argued that there are two complementary postmodern utopias: that of the wondrous healing capacity of the free market, and that of the infinite capacity of the 'technological fix'. There is also, in the fast capitalist literature, a certain 'sci/tech determinism'—if a new technology exists it must be immediately exploited in a highly competitive world or someone else will use it to their advantage. Neither utopian nor determinist views leave much space for reflection on the effects of technology.

One major issue—raised by, for example, Aronowitz and DiFazio (1994)—concerns the effects of science and technology on the distribution of knowledge and power in society. Fast capitalist literature often writes in glowing terms about the elevating and empowering effect of knowledge for the new 'knowledge workers' in 'knowledge societies'. However, Aronowitz and DiFazio, through case studies, argue that in many areas science and technology pool higher order knowledge into ever smaller and more powerful groups of people—the people who understand and manipulate the science and technology—and deskill a great many others, including many 'professionals'.

For example, as computer programs take over much of the work of drafting and design in engineering and architecture, low-level professional workers know less, with their expertise more and more an artefact of their manipulation of the machine. Those who design and program the technology know more and have more flexibility and power in their work. They become a sort of arcane priesthood within the profession. The same sorts of things have been happening in medicine and law, as well as a great number of other areas. The issue is a commonplace on the factory floor—where the mere fact that workers are tending technology does not mean that they really understand it or can control it. In a knowledge society there needs to be a renewed and vigorous debate about what sorts of knowledge bring flexibility and power, and what sorts do not.

We do not intend here to take a definitive position on the vexed issue of whether technology *in general* deskills people or not. The fact of the matter is that the effects of technology—just like the effects of literacy—are *context- and practice-specific* (Hutchins 1995). Technology and technological changes do what they do only in relation to the specific contexts, practices, cultures, and Discourses in which they are used. The point is, however, that fast capitalist texts—much like traditional universalist views of literacy—look at science and technology in quite non-context-specific ways. However, there is a dawning realization in the fast capitalist literature itself that some companies have suffered serious losses by relying too heavily on technology to fix their problems.

The key issue here is whether and how, in specific cases, distributed knowledge, technology, and newly designed social processes either liberate people's creativity or close it down, leaving higher order thinking to a small caste of 'priests' and 'leaders'. Our case study of workers in an electronic assembly plant, in Chapters 4 and 5, bears on these and related issues.

2. The second feature is that the new capitalism is characterized by 'an ever growing role' being played in the organization of work and the enhancement of productivity by 'the manipulation of symbols' (Castells 1993: 17). In the new work order we find a pronounced trend away from material production and toward information-processing activities. Not only is a greater and greater proportion of developed countries' GNP accounted for by trade in 'data, words, oral and visual representations' (Reich 1992: 177), but a greater and greater proportion of the workforce is employed in such activities, either as 'foot soldiers of the information economy . . . stationed in "back offices" at computer terminals linked to worldwide information banks' (ibid: 175) or as 'symbolic analysts' involved in the higher order problem solving. According to Castells, the quality of the information and efficiency in acquiring and processing it 'now constitute the strategic factor in both

competitiveness and productivity for firms, regions, and countries' (1993: 17–18).

There is no doubt that symbols and information are major themes, as well, in the fast capitalist literature. In fact, fast capitalist texts stress that everyone in the organization—including the customer—needs to be an 'insider' privy to nearly all the information the organization has, and to share information openly and freely. There is, too, a mania of collecting as much information as possible on customers, as well as monitoring and measuring worker performance and efficiency continuously and copiously—for development, not evaluation (it is claimed).

The fast capitalist literature is, by and large, silent on the intrusiveness of this information sharing and gathering and on the ways in which it is used to position people and create new social identities. Additionally, in an information-rich world the skill that becomes crucial is not *getting* information (that becomes trivial) but *filtering* and *assessing* it. Once again, we are in danger of a world in which those who can filter and assess are 'priests' and the rest of us merely givers and consumers of information, information valued for the ways in which it can be manipulated, not for its 'truth'.

One interesting and important feature of new information technologies is that they progressively collapse the distinction between workers *doing* a job using the technology and the technology *monitoring* and *evaluating* the job they are doing. Both processes occur almost simultaneously and in complex interaction with one another. The goal is to improve the worker's performance through immediate feedback as well as to continuously feed evaluative information to 'bosses'. As workers and leaders both receive nearly simultaneous feedback, distinctions between doing a job and learning more about it, and between developmental evaluation and judgmental assessment, also begin to collapse. It is easy to see the ways in which information can be abused in such a system—information and feedback become the speeded-up 'assembly line' that drives the knowledge worker's performance. The 'empowered' worker—ever monitored by his or her tools and technologies—is in danger of becoming the victim of a new high-tech panopticon.

At a deeper level, the fast capitalist world is a *semiotic* world, a world of signs and symbols, a world where 'design' and 'life *style*' count more than the materiality of products or the concrete social practices of people and institutions. What Lyotard (1988) said of the 'modern project' becomes all the more true: '. . . humanity is divided into two parts. One confronts the challenge of complexity, the other confronts the ancient, terrible challenge of survival.' For some people the world becomes a rich tapestry to be read for all its 'play of signifiers' (Baudrillard 1988; Derrida 1976); for others guns and bullets are not most important as 'signifiers' but as things that rip apart bodies and communities. It is here that the avant garde academic, whatever his or her politics, makes deepest contact with the new capitalism: they both celebrate signs and symbols, and their manipulation, as the most important part of or even as constitutive of 'reality'—a luxury that, as we will see below, many in the new work order may not have.

3. A third feature that Castells points to is that the new capitalism reflects dramatic changes from the old capitalism in the ways in which production and other economic processes are organized. This, it transpires, is the feature most heavily stressed in the fast capitalist storyline. Hierarchy is reduced among employees; borders are eased between businesses (e.g. producers and suppliers) and business units. Decentralization, networking, flexibility, cooperation, collaboration, customization getting close to the customer, and small, flexible, and local organization—these indeed are major motifs of the fast capitalist literature.

Let's consider the principles of 'small' and 'local', which are especially interesting in light of the globalism of the new capitalism. Listen in this regard, once again, to Tom Peters:

> 'I think I figured out why all these little businesses work. They've got to.' From that comment was born what I call the 'gotta unit' concept.
>
> A gotta unit is one of modest size, which may be living in a larger body but which routinely does the impossible, not because its members read books (even mine) on getting close to the customer, but for precisely the reason the mom-and-pop grocery store will do almost anything (and then some) to serve its neighbors in the surrounding seven-block area. Without that effort, it goes out of business. Kaput. In other words, they do it, cause they gotta.
>
> Implementing the gotta concept almost amounts to automating spunk—making it absolutely necessary for the unit to deliver a spirited response to every customer (Peters 1994: 45).

Ironically, then, despite (but in reality because of) the 'global dreams' of the new capitalism (Barnet & Cavanagh 1994), the fast capitalist world becomes a quite closed world of 'local' and 'personal' relationships. The big corporation disappears, only to show up in the guise of 'mom and pop', just 'one of us' on the local scene. However, mom and pop are forced to behave according to the dictates of the new fast capitalist world—not by social forces but by customers, who are, in fact, their friends in the neighborhood. This is the 'consumer determinism' of the fast capitalist literature to which we return below. And yet Peters is, in the quote above, talking about the 50- to 200-person units of a $3 billion financial services company (the Associated Group of Indianapolis).

Of course, this localism allows corporations to shed old 'nation state' identities and merge with the local coloring, however it is defined (whether in ethnic, religious, class, gender, territorial, or other terms). Peters' personalized and local 'gotta units' often represent imperial corporations operating in terms of a new global order (Barnet & Cavanagh 1994). History, politics, society, and economics disappear, replaced by the personal relationship between mom and pop and their customers.

The social and personal become, in fact, for fast capitalist texts, a domain of scientific and technological manipulation: the term 'sociotechnical' as in 'sociotechnical designs' and 'sociotechnical practices', is common. Just as a business needs cutting-edge technology for success, it also needs to design and engineer social processes and relationships to best effect—for efficiency, information sharing, and total commitment. In the next chapter we will see that distributing knowledge across members of a team is a core sociotechnical device and a leading edge of business influence on educational reform.

The point here is that what fast capitalist texts treat as sociotechnical aspects of organizational design—things like quality circles, project teams, and the integration of technology into work processes—have deep implications for social relations (see Chapters 4 and 5 for a concrete example). The fast capitalist world is one that celebrates temporary and fast-changing networks, whether of co-workers or different businesses. The networks come together for a given project and disperse into other configurations as projects, products, and services change in the hypercompetitive and fast-paced environment of the new capitalism. The fast capitalist literature is silent about the implications of these ephemeral networks for stable communities of people with shared histories and long-term commitments (other than to the vision and core values of the organization). Consider Peters again:

> I like the word 'ephemeral' almost as much as 'fashion' or 'fickle.' In fact, I'm fond of speaking of 'the four ephemerals': ephemeral organizations . . . joined in ephemeral combinations . . . producing ephemeral products . . . for ephemeral markets . . . FAST (Peters 1992: 15–18).

We have every right to ask—a matter we consider further below—what the basis of morality is in a world in which being 'ephemeral' is a high value.

4. A fourth feature of the new capitalism is that competition and the market are now global. An individual worker's competition is no longer just another person looking for a job but, rather, entire labor markets abroad. What holds for the worker holds equally for the corporation. It is simply no longer possible to think of a national economy or national companies in the manner of earlier times. This has far-reaching implications for workers in the new work order:

> [W]hen an 'American' company like General Motors shows healthy profits, this is good news for its strategic brokers in Detroit and its American investors. It is also good news for other GM executives worldwide and for GM's global employees, subcontractors, and investors. But it is not necessarily good news for a lot of routine assembly-line workers in Detroit, because there are not likely to be many of them left in Detroit, or anywhere else in America (Reich 1992: 172).

Reich has written most eloquently about the social and moral implications of this new (because greatly expanded) globalism. Elites who control information and culture share more in cultural and aesthetic values with their peers across the developed world than they do with their less advantaged fellow citizens. While these fellow citizens get progressively worse off as an effect of the new global hypercompetitive capitalism, what could cause the new global elites to feel any moral or social obligation to them? The notion of a civic space in which different classes and groups of people share responsibilities with and to each other is seriously eroded. Perhaps the threat of revolution and violence alone could motivate the elites, though they might well take recourse to guarded-gate communities, increased policing, and movement to various safe havens across the world.

The fast capitalist literature rarely confronts seriously or directly the issue of globalization and its effects on civic spaces and non-market-driven notions of local community. The reason for this is that the fast capitalist literature is deeply devoted to what we call 'consumer determinism'. These texts lead one to believe that all the effects of the new capitalism are caused, not by complex economic, technological, and global issues, and certainly not by the compounding effects of greed and technology, but *by consumers' desires*. The consumer is seen as the transformative agent and cause of our current economic upheavals:

> *Question*: Why are companies putting themselves through all
> this radical (not to mention agonizing) change?
> *Answer*: Because customers are demanding quick,
> customized solutions to their problems, and smart
> companies are reinventing themselves to meet their
> demands (Peters 1994: 45).

Peters' view is all-pervasive in the fast capitalist literature. The focus on customer-as-agent-of-change forms a consumer determinism to replace 'old fashioned' economic determinism centered on the forces of production. In fact, the fast capitalist literature is concerned not with production, the focus of much Marxist literature, but with productivity defined as the *value* added to the enterprise by each worker/partner, where value is ultimately spelt out as providing quality for the customer or completely meeting the customer's specifications (Crosby 1979). This concern, of course, manages to efface various social, political, cultural, and economic forces changing our world and to render the search for ever greater 'perfection' necessary, inevitable, and unavoidable (and, since *we* are the customer, it would be to cheat ourselves to offer anything short of the best).

Zygmunt Bauman has pointed out that one of the distinctions between modernism and old capitalism, on the one hand, and postmodernism and new capitalism, on the other, is that the former deemed itself *universal*, while the latter thinks of itself instead as *global*.

> Behind the change of terms hides a watershed in the history of
> modern self-awareness and self-confidence. Universal was to be the
> rule of reason—the order of things that would replace slavery to
> passions with the autonomy of rational beings, superstition and
> ignorance with truth, tribulations of the drifting plankton with
> self-made and thoroughly monitored history-by-design. 'Globality',
> in contrast, means merely that everyone everywhere may feed on
> McDonald's burgers and watch the latest made-for-TV docudrama
> (Bauman 1992: 24).

The old capitalism was about *commodities*. By commodities we mean standardized products sold to large numbers of people who must themselves become standardized. In fact, in the old capitalism this standardization was seen by many as a good thing. For example, in the United States the sociologist Franklin Giddings argued in 1922 that standardization was the key to integrating America's diverse population into a unified whole (see Leach 1993: 243). The idea was that if Americans desired the same goods and dreamed the same dreams there would be nothing to fear from anarchists. Giddings argued that people who want the same things and who have the same tastes would 'exhibit mental and moral solidarity' (ibid: 243).

The old capitalism was, then, we might say, about 'democratizing desire' (ibid: 3)—that is, unifying people through unifying desire. The old capitalism believed that democracy requires solidarity of a sort that transcends subgroup and individual interests. It saw standardized consumption as the basis—in fact, the *moral basis*—for this solidarity.

The new capitalism as defined in the fast capitalist literature is not about commodities or standardization, and very probably not about democracy. The new capitalism is, as we have seen, about *customization*: the design of products and services perfectly dovetailed to the needs, desires, and identities of individuals on the basis of their *differences*. These differences may be rooted in their various sub-group affiliations or in their unique individuality.

Thus the new capitalism celebrates diversity and abhors standardization. The new capitalism is not about democratizing desire, but rather about customizing desire. In Bauman's words the new capitalism has nothing to gain from what the old capitalism promoted—things like 'strict and universal *rules*' and 'unambiguous criteria of *truth, morality and beauty*'. Bauman goes on to say that 'the powers-that-be lost, so to speak, all interest in universally binding standards . . . ' (1992: 52).

Both the old capitalism and the new have a more benign side and a more sinister side, though the two capitalisms are something like mirror images of each other. In the case of the old capitalism, we can applaud the valuing of democracy and solidarity. But we must regret that these were to be based on standardization and consumption. In the case of the new capitalism, we can applaud the valuing of diversity as against enforced assimilation. But we must regret that diversity is, in the new capitalism, often a customized artefact of high-tech marketing. Furthermore, assimilation is achieved at a 'higher' level by allegiance to 'core values' and/or 'visionary leadership' over which one has little say.

The dark sides of the two capitalisms require different forms of critique. And, in fact, we have yet to fully invent an adequate language of critique for the new capitalism. As we have seen, it won't do to critique the new capitalism on the basis of its desires to universalize the standards of middle class white culture. While the new capitalism may well aim to further enrich this group, it does not desire everyone to consume or aspire to the same products and identities. The new capitalism is based on a very different form of hegemony than the old.

IV Dysutopia in the new capitalism

There is a core social problem of the world that the new capitalism is bringing into being, a problem that is virtually ignored in the fast capitalist literature (with an important exception which we mention below). We are heading towards a world in which a small number of countries and a small number of people within them will benefit substantively from the new capitalism, while a large number of others will be progressively worse off and exploited. When, in the old capitalism, corporations were tied (though never totally) to nation states, the citizens of these nation states stood some chance of benefiting as citizens from the prosperity of the corporations. In a world in which all corporations are global, it is not citizens of this or that state that benefit, but certain globalized classes of people—leaders and 'symbolic analysts' of various sorts.

We have already seen the ways in which the new capitalism encourages the pooling of high-value resources (knowledge and information) into fewer hands. Furthermore, in a capitalism that pays only for 'value added', and where value is largely defined in terms of knowledge, information, design, and symbolic value, much work must perforce go virtually unrewarded. A corpus of 'value adders'—ever smaller as technology advances—gain advantage, while a massive periphery of service providers and temporary workers gain little and work 'on demand'. And, indeed, temporary, part-time, and subcontracted workers have been the fastest growing segment of the workforce over the last few decades (Parker 1994; Reich 1992). Such workers typically have few or no fringe benefits and often cannot collect unemployment benefits. They absorb seasonal or cyclical fluctuations in business activity.

Furthermore, as Castells points out, the new capitalism seems to necessitate that an 'undeveloped' country be exploited as a global periphery source of low cost labor before it can enter the enchanted circle of the new capitalism—and then produce a class of core workers who can, in their turn, exploit peripheral workers both in their country and abroad. In fact, we are witnessing a new sort of moral argument: being exploited for low wages and poor working conditions is better than having no job at all and forms the 'dues' required for undeveloped countries (or Third World enclaves of developed countries) eventually to enter the charmed circle of the new capitalism.

Peripheral workers constitute a massive supply of underemployed and periodically unemployed workers, as will the growing hordes of service workers who sell not knowledge but the brute delivery of services connected to the ever newly designed lifestyles of the 'winners' in the new capitalism. Peter Drucker, one of the senior gurus of fast capitalism, has argued—virtually as a lone voice among fast capitalist authors—that the growing numbers of low-paid service workers (and we can add the underemployed and unemployed in general) will represent the main social 'class' problem of the new capitalism:

> The social challenge of the post-capitalist society will, however, be the dignity of the second class in post-capitalist society: the service workers. Service workers, as a rule, lack the necessary education to be knowledge workers. And in every country, even the most highly advanced one, they will constitute the majority (Drucker 1993: 8).

Peter O'Connor summarizes this paradox of the new capitalism, the large reservoir of disenchanted workers that seems to be a necessary accompaniment of the new enchanted workplace. O'Connor claims that, in order to achieve maximum flexibility:

> . . . companies will increasingly [subcontract] a range of functions, and further reduce and segment their workforce by maintaining a core workforce which is multi-skilled, flexible, and can be used across operational functions, and a peripheral workforce which is more disposable, based on part-time and temporary work, short-term individual contracts and fewer employment rights and entitlements...
>
> [Indeed] the core remains the domain predominantly of men, providing more skill flexibility and development and diverse work, while the periphery is predominantly the domain of women workers, with fewer opportunities and further deskilling and control.
>
> [It is possible that this] 'core–periphery' dualism merely extends and intensifies labor market segregation by gender, race and age, [and that] we may simply be experiencing a switch in management strategies which, rather than delivering democracy and greater opportunity in the workplace, further enhances and extends managerial control (O'Connor 1993: 13–14).

The global perspective on the new-capitalist work order taken by theorists like Castells (1993) and Fernando Henrique Cardoso (1993) accentuates the paradoxical logic of enchanted work leading to a proliferation of disenchanted workers. Castells and Cardoso look beyond local and national levels to reveal an international division of labor characterized by vast inequalities—to the point of possible exclusion of entire national and continental economies from the new world economy.

The theory-driven, value-added, information-based global economy has ushered in an international division of labor reflecting primarily 'the capacity to create new knowledge and apply it rapidly, via information processing and telecommunications, to a wide range of human activities in ever broadening space and time (Carnoy *et al.* 1993: 6). Cardoso argues that large parts of the South (as in the North–South divide—cf Brandt 1980) are becoming increasingly marginal—and potentially irrelevant—to the world economy:

> We are no longer talking about the South that was on the periphery of the capitalist core and was tied to it in a classical relationship of dependence. We are dealing, in truth, with a crueler phenomenon: either the South (or a portion of it) enters the democratic-technological-scientific race, invests heavily in R & D, and endures the 'information economy' metamorphosis, or it becomes unimportant, unexploited, and unexploitable.
>
> [T]hose countries (or parts thereof) which are unable to repeat the revolution of the contemporary world, and at the same time find a niche in the international market, will end up in the 'worst of all possible worlds'. They will not even be considered worth the trouble of exploitation; they will become inconsequential, of no interest to the developing globalized economy (Cardoso 1993: 156).

In Chapter 6 we will look specifically at the attempts of people in a 'less developed country' to survive and cope in a world ruled more and more by the dictates of the new global, high-tech capitalism. In Chapters 4 and 5 we will look at front-line workers in a 'developed country' coping with the same world, though on different terms.

Robert Reich's compelling book, *The Work of Nations (1992)* gives us a good insight into the social problems we are here pointing to. In his Chapter 13 Reich argues that three broad categories of work are emerging across nations in the new world economy. He calls these 'routine production services', 'in-person services', and 'symbolic-analytic services' respectively. Between them they will eventually account for almost all the paid work performed in modern economies. While the percentages in the first two categories are continuing to grow, the proportion of symbolic-analytic workers in the US workforce has become more or less static.

Symbolic-analytic work involves services that are delivered in the form of data, words, and oral and visual representations. It comprises diverse problem-identifying, problem-solving, and strategic brokering activities (Reich 1992: 177). As such, symbolic-analytic services span the work of research scientists, all manner of engineers (from civil to sound), management consultants, investment bankers, systems analysts, authors, editors, art directors, video and film producers, musicians, and so on.

Unlike symbolic-analytic work, much of the work in the first two categories is not seen as being substantial value-adding activity. Furthermore, beyond demands for basic numeracy and the ability to read, such work tends to call primarily for reliability, loyalty, and the capacity to take direction and, in the case of in-person service workers, 'a pleasant demeanor'. Thus there is a vast potential labor pool which is now global. The logistics of labor supply and demand, in conjunction with the perceived low value-adding nature of this work, mean that it is poorly rewarded relative to symbolic-analytic work.

Against this backdrop Reich speaks of a rising one-fifth and a falling four-fifths in the new work order of economies like our own. In highlighting different categories and 'realities' of work, which are either ignored or are at best glossed over by most fast capitalist authors, Reich's account indicates a potential—and increasingly actual—problem of alarming depth and proportion for modern economies. In the end we are arguing that the lean and mean hypercompetitive, perfection-driven nature of the new capitalism requires a core of relatively well paid knowledge leaders and workers supplemented by a bevy of people 'servicing' them for the least possible price so that their ideas can be translated into the highest quality, most competitive products possible. These 'servants', whether in a less developed country or in Third World pockets of developed countries, will merit their lowly places because of their lack of knowledge and education—the new currency of the new capitalism.

Even the recommendation advanced by Reich—investing in promoting the wealth-creating capacities of our compatriots—has a hollow ring. 'Educational reform' in terms of ensuring quality schools for everyone is deeply paradoxical, because if everyone were educated there would be no servants. The new capitalism is in danger of producing and reproducing an even steeper pyramid than the old capitalism did. And, just as in the old capitalism, it will need institutions—like schools, first and foremost—to reproduce that social structure.

Reich suggests that, on the basis of recent and current trends, the futures of the best off and worst off in economies like our own will continue to diverge to the extent that, unless appropriate interventions are enacted, by the year 2020 'the top fifth of American earners will account for more than 60 percent of all the income earned by Americans; the bottom fifth 2 percent' (Reich 1992: 302). As we discussed above in regard to the erosion of civic spaces, Reich develops a yet deeper dimension to this problem in his well-titled chapter, 'Who is 'us'?':

> . . . America's problem is that, while some Americans are adding substantial value, most are not. In consequence, the gap between those few in the first group and everyone else is widening. To improve the economic position of the bottom four-fifths will require that the fortunate fifth share its wealth and invest in the wealth-creating capacities of other Americans. Yet as the top becomes ever more tightly linked to the global economy, it has less stake in the performance and potential of its less fortunate compatriots. Thus our emerging dilemma, and that of other nations as well (Reich 1992: 301).

Any discussion of the new capitalism needs to be framed quite overtly in terms of the sorts of social problems that Reich is pointing to. Otherwise, we are in grave danger of simply promoting the 'hardheaded' utopianism of the fast capitalist literature—where everyone can 'sink or swim' on their own—and of ignoring the fact that very real forces, including the actions of elites, many of them already greatly advantaged by the institutions of the old capitalism, are pushing many people under.

Our purpose in this chapter has been to characterize what we have called the fast capitalist version of the new capitalism and to place it in the wider framework of a social, institutional, and cultural critique. The next chapter deals with the impact of the new capitalism on learning and schools and with its impact on the language of critique itself. Then we turn to two case studies, one involving workers in the United States (Chapters 4 and 5) and the other involving people in a developing country (Chapter 6), all seeking to cope with the real world as it is transformed by the new capitalism. These case studies will give us deeper insights into the nature of knowledge, learning, and literacy—within their wider moral, social, institutional, and cultural frameworks—in our 'new times'.

3 Alignments: education and the new capitalism

Companies come together in temporary alliances to take advantage of a brief window of opportunity and then disband to form yet another configuration of customers, vendors, and suppliers (Imparato and Harari 1994: 167).

. . . the agenda that these users infer from playing these games is that they must learn to see reality as a myriad of interconnections rather than just a few power relationships (Rushkoff 1994: 15, 184).

Postmodern society is radically decentered and thoroughly disseminated. As a result of this dispersion, the machine of socio-cultural reproduction is no longer controlled by centralized agencies. Center and hierarchy give rise to periphery and horizontality . . . (Taylor and Saarinen 1994, Simcult section: 1).

The first quote is about business, the second about computer games, the last about society. Equivalent quotes could be produced about minds, cells, ecosystems, or the weather. Talk of networks, connections, interconnections, and the breakdown of hierarchy is now all-pervasive. The business themes of the previous chapter are, it turns out, part of a larger story. In this chapter we discuss this larger story and its impact on current ideas about learning, knowledge, and school reform. We close the chapter with a brief discussion of the implications for critiques of capitalism. Basically, our claim is this: under the guise of the larger story we tell here there is a growing alignment between the business world in the new capitalism and various non-business spheres of interest, including schools and academic disciplines promoting school reform efforts.

49

I A master story for our new times

Whole swaths of academic disciplines are 'retooling' themselves around a set of common themes. Physics, biology, mathematics, cognitive science, neuroscience, computer science, and economics are all now intensely concerned with unpredictable properties that emerge out of myriad bits and pieces interacting within complex systems. These bits and pieces might be neurons in the developing brain, concepts in creative thinking, vortexes in weather or water, artificial life forms simulated on computers, species evolving in the natural world, values in a marketplace, or numbers in a non-linear equation. Those concerned with media, technology, communication, society, culture, history, and institutions have rebuilt their discourses as well around these new themes (see, among a great many sources, Kauffman 1991; Kelly 1994; Lorentz 1993; Waldrop 1992).

But what, we may ask, is the core idea in all this talk of networks, emergence, complexity, decentering, chaos, interconnections, and fluidity? It is, we believe, this: Lots of people in lots of areas are (in thought and deed) deserting *systems of one type* for *systems of another type*. We are living through a major shift in how our physical, biological, social, and mechanical worlds are viewed, studied, constructed, and worked on. Old-style systems based on authoritarian hierarchy, which we once found—and thought we wanted—in the mind, in nature, in society, and in organizations, are 'out'. Such systems involve a (small) top controlling a (bigger) middle controlling a (yet larger) bottom in a top-down, linear flow of hierarchical and pyramidal power and information.

'In' are systems with 'non-authoritarian hierarchy', a fitting oxymoron for our new age. In such systems many small, efficient, and self-controlled local units act in fluid, flexible, and sometimes ephemeral combinations while being *assisted* by a 'top' that cannot directly control them, nor fully understand them and their actions. Furthermore, this new 'top' functions (paradoxically) both inside and outside the system of interacting units—like an 'outside world' (sometimes it actually *is* the outside world) which the units act on, get responses from, and 'consult' until they eventually become symbiotically integrated with it and adapted to it. Note that in new capitalist businesses this 'top' is sometimes the boss/coach, sometimes the consumer and/or the market, and sometimes both.

Molecules in a flowing liquid are a clear example of just such a non-authoritarian hierarchy—ephemeral but functional combinations of molecules arise fluidly and adaptably in response to environmental feedback and assistance from inside and outside the liquid system; so, too, are the now oft-celebrated 'flat hierarchies' in the new capitalism. Nor is it surprising that the global flow of money, products, ideas, populations, or tourists is a key notion in contemporary economic and sociological theories (Lash and Urry 1994).

We will refer to such non-authoritarian hierarchies as 'distributed systems', because, in them, control is distributed throughout the system, and not centered in any 'center' that monopolizes power, knowledge, or control. Distributed systems have become a *leitmotif* of late twentieth century life because of exponential growth in *variety*, *variability*, and *diversity* of all sorts in all areas. Technological and social (e.g. demographic) changes in a global world have caused us to focus on systems in which variables, interactions, relationships, and complexity are nearly 'out of control', but in which emerging patterns can sometimes be harnessed or 'leveraged' for productive thought, work, and change. But they can only be so leveraged through new ways of thinking and acting that disown an older linear logic we previously valued in our thinking, (thought we) found everywhere in the world (thanks, for instance, to Newtonian physics), and built into our organizations.

Before we move to more specific concerns with businesses and schools, let us give a very simple example of the sort of 'intelligence' and control found in distributed systems. Consider, in this regard, a collection robot (actually it is called a 'mobot') designed to collect empty soda cans in a lab at MIT (see Kelly 1994: 34–49; the mobot was designed by R. A. Brooks). The mobot has no 'central brain', but rather 'intelligence' and decision-making capacities distributed throughout its mechanical body. It simply roams around until its video camera spots the shape of a soda can on a desk. This signal triggers the wheels of the mobot and propels it in front of the can. Rather than wait for a message from a central brain, the arm of the robot 'learns' where it is from the environment. The arm is wired so that it 'looks' at its wheels. If it 'sees' that its wheels are not turning, it 'knows' that it must be in front of a soda can. The arm then reaches out to pick up the can. If the can is heavier than an empty can, it is left on the desk. If it is light, the mobot (the arm?—whose act is this anyway?) takes it. The mobot then roams (not bumping into furniture or walls because of its avoidance module) until it comes across the recycling station. Then it stops its wheels in front of the station. The arm 'looks' at its hand to see if it is holding a can; if it is, it drops it. If there is no can in its hand, it begins to wander again through the offices until it spots another can.

This mobot has a very different sort of 'intelligence' than we are used to. It has 'smart parts' that interact and no central boss other than the world to which it is adapting and the scientists that designed and mediated its relationship to that world. This mobot is interesting not because it itself represents a very complex system but rather because it demonstrates that distributing control across many parts, rather than in a central 'brain', can lead to a system that behaves as if it has some centralized intelligence,—when in fact it doesn't. It also saves the immense cost, in both money and weight, of building a central brain. With a central, all-knowing, all-controlling brain the mobot's head, it turns out, would be so heavy that the mobot could not carry it around (it would have to sit on a desk directing the mobot from afar).

Note, too, that the world itself serves as part of the mobot's 'intelligence'. The soda can on the desk, as well as its weight, and the recycling station all help to structure the mobot's intelligence and behavior. Since recyclable soda cans are lighter than full ones, there is no need for the mobot to have a 'full theory' of recycling in regard to soda cans. It need only have an arm that 'knows' heavy when it feels it. The rest comes free by being represented (actually, continually re-presented) in the world, not in any central brain. In a fast-changing world it is even more important to let the world 're-present' itself and to design the mobot to learn and adapt flexibly and quickly.

Bees, molecules, cells and bodies, the modules of the mind/brain, and markets and organizations in a global world behave this way: lots of self-controlled units relate in a system through feedback and adaptation in such a way that the system looks and acts intelligent. The more complex such a system is the more we are tempted to think that it has (or needs) some central controlling intelligence somewhere. The moral of the 'grand theme' we have been discussing is that this is not so, not so in our brains, not so in nature, and not so in our organizations.

Distributed systems—with complex interactions, flexible adaptation to the 'outside world', and little top-down control—constitute now, and will progressively do so in the future, a grand theme around which alignments across various domains (e.g. business, science, politics, and schools) can and will emerge.

II Business and cognitive science

We have tried to make it clear that the new ways in which new-capitalist businesses and organizations are being talked about are now of a piece with the new ways in which molecules, cells, brains, physical systems, institutions, and societies—indeed, complex systems across the board—are being talked about. Out of this huge mix we discuss here only two specific cases of the intermingling of words, images, and themes between the new capitalism and other spheres of interest. One case (our longer excursion) involves what we might call 'the science of schooling', as well as the very idea of what constitutes learning and knowledge, and the other case (a briefer trip) involves capitalism and its critics.

The previous chapter told the fast-capitalist version of the new-capitalist story. This story essentially centers on the consequences of global hypercompetition coupled with ever more sophisticated scientific and technological advances. In fact, we are entering a world in which businesses are fast becoming distributed systems. In the 'ideal' business, local units (both individuals and small business units) control their own actions, combining and uncombining in flexible ways with other units on demand; the 'intelligence' of the system as a whole is distributed across multiple interrelated units and shaped by the presentations and re-presentations of the customer and the market. The system develops a symbiotic relation to the customer and the market such that it is not merely shaped by it but shapes it as well, a symbiotic relationship that is mediated and facilitated by the 'leader', who cannot control or fully understand the local units but can assist their learning, organization, combination, and adaptation.

Now we turn to the first case, where we look at specific alignments (centered on the theme of distributed systems) between the new capitalism and another sphere of interest: schools and the science that 'supervises' them. In the United States, the discipline of psychology has traditionally been responsible for developing viewpoints on thinking and learning and translating these into educational practice. Over the last few decades, however, a new 'megadiscipline' has emerged to subsume many of the chores of psychology (Barsalou 1992; Gardner 1985). This megadiscipline is 'cognitive science', an amalgam of psychology, neuroscience, computer science, philosophy, linguistics, and other disciplines, focused on the nature of thinking and intelligence in animal, human, and artificial minds.

Our argument here is not that school reforms inspired by cognitive science are widespread or a major global movement on their own. Rather, we argue that the fundamental features of reform coming out of educationally relevant cognitive science are core aspects of a great many other reform efforts. They just happen to be better 'rationalized' in cognitive science, thanks to its prestige as the 'science of mind'. Such features are fast becoming major motifs of a new 'common sense' about schools and schooling.

Schools in the United States have always had to produce bodies and minds suitable for the world of work. Nonetheless, schools have also represented, at certain times and places, broader and sometimes conflicting interests, such as social justice, cultural integrity, citizenship, and critique. Schooling has historically been a site where complex processes of alignment and dis-alignment with other forces in the society—e.g. business, government, ethnic groups, and the family—are at work.

At the same time, an academic discipline like cognitive science, which seeks to control curricula and pedagogy in schools, has complex interests of its own. These (historically changing) interests partly resonate and partly conflict with the interests of other sectors, such as business, churches, government, the public sphere, media and, indeed, teachers and schools, all of which can broadly be seen as competing to 'educate' people and to define what counts as knowledge, at least knowledge worth having.

It is our contention that contemporary, educationally relevant cognitive science, and many related school reform efforts, are in the process of aligning themselves more and more with the themes and interests of the new capitalism. (It is not our concern here whether this alignment is consciously done or not—that is another story for another time.)

Let us, then, turn to the ways in which cognitive science is coming to produce 'new minds' better attuned to the interests of the new capitalism. The story as we tell it here has two parts: first, what constitutes 'knowledge' and 'real understanding' (dealt with in this section) and, second, the nature of control, goals, and values in distributed systems, whether these be new classrooms or new workplaces (dealt with in the following section).

First, knowledge and understanding. Contemporary cognitive science has replaced an earlier critique of schools, based on the disproportionate failure of many lower socioeconomic and minority students, with a new and initially rather startling critique: that it's not just minorities who fail, in actuality nearly all students do (Bruer 1993; Gardner 1991). Even those with good grades do not 'really understand' what they are learning. Students in traditional schools, it is claimed, master only basic, rote, low-level skills, at best. While such students may be able to pass tests and carry out basic computations, they really do not understand, in any very deep way, what they are doing.

It is interesting that the new capitalism offers much the same critique of traditional workers in the old top-down, hierarchically oriented capitalism. Workers could do what they were told, but they did not understand their jobs or the organizations in which they worked well enough to take proactive responsibility for true problem-solving or to feel truly committed to the organization. These two symmetrical critiques are, we would argue, part of the process of alignment between the two projects.

It is over the issue of what constitutes 'real understanding' that we can best trace current processes of alignment between cognitive science and the new capitalism. The story is tellable in quick strokes if we look at a few programmatic statements from leading educational cognitive scientists.

In 1991 Howard Gardner diagnosed the problem with today's students and proposed the solution to the problem in what had by then become, in cognitive science circles, canonical terms. The problem, as Gardner saw it, is that education does not remove or correct people's everyday 'folk theories', and people readily fall back on these folk theories even when they have been, or are being, exposed in school to 'correct', or at least 'better', theories based on disciplines. Even if they can answer school tests correctly, their school-based knowledge falls apart in the face of their well-entrenched, but unexamined, folk theories when they are moved to a slightly different problem or, worse yet, to a new, (but related) domain. Only 'experts'—people who really understand' the disciplinary theories—can avoid this, and so, what schools must do is produce students who learn to think and act like disciplinary experts. This, then, is the solution. For Gardner, to think well, to 'really understand', is to think like a disciplinary specialist:

> . . . the *disciplinary expert* (or skilled person) [is] an individual of any age who has mastered the concepts and skills of a discipline or domain and can apply such knowledge appropriately in new situations. Included in the ranks of the disciplinary experts are those students who are able to use the knowledge of their physics class or their history class to illuminate new phenomena. Their knowledge is not limited to

the usual text-and-test setting, and they are eligible to enter the ranks of those who 'really' understand (Gardner 1991: 7).

Gardner's work represents the end point of a major shift in cognitive psychology and cognitive science that took place over several decades: a shift from thinking of thinking in general terms—'good thinking' versus 'bad thinking'—to thinking of thinking in domain-specific terms (see Barsalou 1992; Bruer 1993; Perkins 1995 for overviews). Cognitive psychologists had come to believe that there was no such thing as 'good thinking' in general; rather, good thinking was tied to deep experience of specific domains (e.g. academic disciplines) and differed from domain to domain. The catchphrase 'less is more' became popular in school reform efforts: learning in depth about a limited area leads to more 'intelligence' than learning a little about a lot, which could only be based on hopes of somehow making real the chimera of 'generic good thinking'.

In the old authoritarian, hierarchical capitalism the expertise of the specialist was highly valued. Indeed, 'management' was itself a type of disciplinary expertise (Kotter 1995) created by and learned in business schools (themselves very much creatures of the old capitalism). But such expertise is best suited to supervising and disciplining others less knowledgeable than oneself in static times in which knowledge has a long 'shelf life'. The new capitalism focuses on change, flexibility, speed, and innovation. In this context disciplinary expertise goes out of date too rapidly and central controlling forms of intelligence are too big and too slow:

> Once we feel as if we have 'the answer', all motivation to question our thinking disappears. But the discipline of systems thinking shows that there simply is 'no right answer' when dealing with complexity . . .
>
> The 'compartmentalization of knowledge' creates a false sense of confidence. For example, the traditional disciplines that influence management—such disciplines as economics, accounting, marketing, and psychology—divide the world into neat subdivisions within which one can often say, 'This is the problem and here is the solution'. But the boundaries that make the subdivisions are fundamentally arbitrary—as any manager finds out who attempts to treat an important problem as if it is purely 'an economic problem' or 'an accounting problem'. Life comes to us whole. It is only the analytic lens we impose that makes it seem as if problems can be isolated and solved. When we forget that it is 'only a lens', we lose the spirit of openness (Senge 1991: 281, 283).

Gardner made his claims in a popular book that captured the mainstream view at the time: to think well is to have in one's head the same sorts of mental representations as a disciplinary expert (see also Bruer 1993). However, of late, cognitive science has progressively shifted its notion of expertise away from disciplinary or academic expertise to a broader notion more compatible with the worldview of the new capitalism. This has constituted something of a cautious return to a more generalist approach to 'good thinking'. For example, Carl Bereiter and Marlene Scardamalia, two cognitive scientists of Gardner's rank, have recently rendered the convergence of cognitive science and the new capitalism closer and more overt. Bereiter and Scardamalia (1993) distinguish between expertise and 'specialization' (p. 6) and clearly divorce the two. They see expertise as a *process*, not a product, a process involving a 'continual reinvestment of mental resources into addressing problems at higher levels' (p. 221). People, they say, 'must become expert at becoming experts' (p. 2) by developing the ability to work in non-routine ways on ever more demanding problems in whatever domain they are confronted with.

Here we get a contrast very like that between the old-style capitalist worker engaged in the mindless routine tasks of the Fordist economy and the new-capitalist worker/partner engaged in a meaningful job and progressively learning and improving performance. It is also typical of the new capitalism to focus on processes and reengineering of processes rather than on divisions, boundaries, and borders (e.g., Lipnack & Stamps 1993).

By the end of their book Bereiter and Scardamalia connect their ideas directly to the notion of 'quality' that plays such a prominent role in the new capitalism:

Although 'quality' is no easier to define than 'excellence', and in everyday language means approximately the same thing, the quality movement has given the idea substance. As conceived by W. Edwards Deming and other gurus of the movement, quality bears a very close resemblance to the concept of expertise that we have been trying to develop here. It is a continuing process, not a state or outcome. It involves all the members of an organization cooperating in pursuit of an ideal goal that can never be attained, but that can be approached endlessly. Although not identified as such, progressive problem solving seems to be implicit in the idea . . .

So close is the resemblance of quality improvement to the process of expertise, that we might even characterize it as the

process of expertise translated into a practical program for
organizations (1993: 242–43).

The same sort of progression can be seen also in the work of David
Perkins, an equally renowned colleague of Gardner's at Harvard's
Project Zero. Perkins (1995) distinguishes between three traditional
approaches to what constitutes 'intelligent behavior': good information
processing ('high IQ'); lots of experience (e.g. disciplinary expertise
of the sort that Gardner extolled); and 'reflective intelligence', which
Perkins champions. Using an analogy to a riverboat pilot, Perkins states
his view of intelligence as follows:

> But the master river pilot benefits from much more than efficient
> information processing [high IQ] and knowledge of the landscape
> [experience and disciplinary expertise]. The master pilot stands alert
> to possible changes, takes a strategic view of time and weather,
> works through choices about route and schedule with the costs and
> benefits in mind. And it's the same with people who pilot their
> minds well—who, to use another common phrase, are good mental
> managers (1995: 99).

Perkins' view of intelligence is stated—albeit in what he intends as
figurative language—in almost entirely business-oriented terms. For
Perkins, there *are* general thinking strategies that cut across and transcend specific domains of inquiry and expertise. His view of reflective,
strategic intelligence as the goal of schooling is entirely in keeping
with the goals of the new capitalism with its emphasis on efficient
problem solving, productivity, innovation, adaptation, and non-authoritarian distributed systems.

The convergence is certainly not yet finished (nor will it ever be
complete). In his more recent work, Bereiter (1994) has begun to
question the 'mental', 'internal', and 'individual' focus of schooling (the
idea that 'mental representation' is or has been heretofore a core notion
of cognitive science). In the new capitalism it is not really important
what individuals know on their own, but rather what they can do with
others in a collaborative way to effectively add 'value' to the enterprise.

Remember, the focus of the new capitalism is on *distributed
systems*. Knowledge and productivity should be distributed across
teams and units; they need not reside inside any one entity that uniquely
controls the process. In fact, if they did reside too heavily inside
individuals those individuals could take their knowledge and 'walk',
selling it to the highest bidder—a real fear in the new knowledge-driven
capitalism. Remember, too, our robot (mobot): there we saw that even

relatively 'dumb' parts add up to a 'smart' system, but a system wherein no one unit contains a 'central' and 'higher' intelligence all by itself. Whether we are talking about work teams or business units or even networked businesses, what matters is the knowledge ('core competencies') distributed across the whole system.

In light of the distributed nature of knowledge and work in the new capitalism, it is interesting to watch Bereiter distinguish between 'learning', where the goal is to change and assess individual minds (the traditional goal of schooling), and 'knowledge building':

> [Knowledge building's] . . . objective is not to influence the contents of students' minds but to produce immaterial objects—explanations, theories, solutions, algorithms. Students are expected to learn something in the process, and this may well be evaluated at some time. But the actual work is not directed toward improving their minds but toward *improving the knowledge* that is being collectively created. The important point, however, is that their focus is outward, on the objects themselves and the world they relate to, rather than on their own mental states or social roles. They feel a kinship with scholars and scientists, but it is a kinship based on shared goals, not on similarities of practice (Bereiter 1994: 23).

Here we see a movement away from schooling as reproducing the identities and practices of disciplinary experts, away even from schooling as producing individually 'smart people'. We see, rather, a movement towards people who can work collaboratively (in teams) to produce results and add value through distributed knowledge and understanding. Such students are much better suited to be parts of a smart mobot, better suited to be modules in a distributed non-authoritarian system, than are traditional students.

And we see similar elements of two domains beginning to align in interests, goals, and perspectives, though not without a struggle. Again, the language and viewpoints have worn smooth so quickly that we might not stop to think that the *goals* of school reformers *could have* been different from, and at various points contesting with, the goals of the new capitalism or of any other market scheme.

III Goals, values, and control

Non-authoritarian distributed systems run into the problem of what will make the units work in the service of the whole. Such systems are always on the border of being 'out of control'—this is part of what, in fact, makes them so powerful (Kelly 1994). Ants in an ant colony behave in the interests of the colony because evolution has seen to it that they 'buy into' those interests without 'knowing' it: in fact, they are built so that following their 'own' interests amounts to following the colony's interests. But what plays the role of evolution in the case of our new colony-like distributed businesses and classrooms? The problem is stressed repeatedly in new-capitalist literature:

> In *Workplace 2000*, rigid hierarchies will be dismantled, as will the ceremonial trappings of power. Egalitarianism will become utilitarian. The goal will be to create among the work force, and between workers and managers, harmony and unity. More importantly, the goal will be to attach people mentally and emotionally to the workplace—to make them feel intimately connected to the corporation even if in reality that connection is transitory (Boyett & Conn 1992: 109).

In the new capitalism there are two competing answers to this problem, as we discussed in earlier chapters. One answer is new-style visionary leadership and the other is the creation of core values as part and parcel of a business's core culture, the internalization of which ensures that everyone will work in the best interests of the organization as a whole.

Both these answers involve forms of 'indirect control' through the arrangement of environments which themselves, in a sense, encode control. Such an approach can easily take on the tones of manipulation. This is what we will call the *core dilemma* of the new capitalism: how to 'control' empowered 'partners' in the absence of visible, overt top-down power. It turns out that classrooms inspired by cognitive science run into just the same dilemma. Furthermore, cognitive scientists have a particularly attractive solution to the problem, one that is quite compatible with the new capitalism.

In fact, we would argue, such classrooms may become the sites at which the new capitalism will seek to solve its core dilemma, at least initially. Such new classrooms may very well progressively produce students pre-equipped to work harmoniously in distributed systems by internalizing core values, values that issue from the social practices and organizational structures of the system itself and not from any visible controlling center.

To make our point quite specific here, let us consider one of the most successful, and most widely publicized, recent classroom applications of cognitive science, a project directed by Ann Brown and Joseph Campione and their colleagues at the University of California at Berkeley (see Brown 1994; unspecified page references given below are to Brown et al. 1993). Brown and Campione create 'learning communities' based on the idea that knowledge does not reside privately in individual heads but rather is situated in activities and distributed, or as Lave (1988: 1) puts it, 'stretched over—not divided among—mind, body, activity and culturally organized settings (which include other actors)'. This is, of course, precisely our theme of distributed systems.

Brown and Campione have, like Bereiter and Scardamalia, deserted the earlier goal of 'disciplinary thinking'. It is 'clearly romantic' to suggest 'that students in public schools be enculturated into the cultures of mathematicians, historians, and literary critics', they argue (189). Rather, schools 'should be communities where students learn to learn' and become 'prepared as life-long learners who have learned how to learn in many domains' (190).

Brown and Campione's classrooms use a wide variety of devices to ensure that knowledge and understanding are public, collaborative, and distributed. Two of these are reciprocal teaching and the 'jigsaw method'. Reciprocal teaching (Brown and Palincsar 1989) is a method of rendering reading comprehension skills (usually thought of as the preserve of 'private minds') public, overt, and distributable. The teacher and a group of students take turns leading a discussion about a reading passage. The leader begins by *asking a question*. The group rereads the passage and discusses possible problems of interpretation when necessary. Attempts to *clarify* any comprehension problems occur opportunistically. At the end of the discussion, the leader *summarizes* the gist of what has been read. The leader also asks for *predictions* about future content. These four skills—questioning, clarifying, summarizing, and predicting—are the core components of successful reading comprehension as cognitive science has uncovered them. Here they are rendered public and overt. Within the context of these reciprocal reading groups, students with varying levels of skill and expertise can participate as they differentially draw on (or 'appropriate') the expertise overtly displayed by other members of the group. Much as in 'quality circles' in the new capitalism, 'units' are made to publicly display and share their knowledge for the benefit of the group (and the system as a whole).

In the jigsaw method of cooperative learning (Aronson 1978) students are assigned a part of a classroom topic to learn and subsequently teach to others via reciprocal teaching. In Brown and Campione's extrapolation of this method the setting is a science classroom. Students do collaborative research in research groups, where each group is devoted to a different subtopic of an overall topic like animal defence mechanisms, changing populations, or food chains. Then they redistribute themselves into learning groups in which each student (using the reciprocal teaching method) takes a turn teaching the other members of her learning group about the subtopic she mastered in her research group.

In the jigsaw method each group or team is expert on only one part of the whole topic; no team is expert on the whole. Each team distributes its knowledge to the whole. There is no single 'leader' (teacher), but each unit (student) plays the role of researcher, student, and teacher in different configurations and contexts. There is no 'center', only a flexible network of distributed roles and responsibilities.

There are many more features of Brown and Campione's classrooms, including a pervasive use of modern computer, telecommunications, and network technologies, that render them much like new-capitalist workplaces. However, all elements of their classrooms are put in place to subserve what we take to be both the crucial concept behind their classrooms and their most important tie to the new capitalism, namely Vygotsky's (1978) notion of a 'zone of proximal development'. It is this notion that allows Brown and Campione to offer, whether or not they realise it, a solution to what we are calling the core dilemma of the new capitalism.

A zone of proximal development is a 'region of activity that learners can navigate with aid from a supporting context, including but not limited to people' (Brown et al. 1993: 191), though they could not yet accomplish such activities on their own. 'It defines the distance between current levels of comprehension and levels that can be accomplished in collaboration with people or powerful artefacts' (191). Students 'lean on' the cognition of others and the knowledge built into artefacts, technologies, and organizational settings before they can operate more 'on their own'. For this to happen, the cognition and knowledge built into such elements needs to be made overt and repeatable, and this is accomplished through the reciprocal teaching and jigsaw techniques as well as the other elements of Brown and Campione's classrooms.

The central idea behind Vygotsky's notion of a zone of proximal development is that novices accomplish with the aid of those more expert than themselves something that they could not bring off on their own. The more expert partner provides a 'scaffold' for the novice by taking up the novice's thoughts, words, and deeds into the expert's own 'activity system', interpreting those thoughts, words, and deeds as if they fit with the expert's understanding of the task, regardless of how the novice might view the situation. In the process novices 'internalize'—without much conscious awareness—the expert's interpretations of what is being accomplished, while progressively gaining the skills needed to act on their own. The beauty of Brown and Campione's classrooms, is that the other students, the various technologies used in the classroom, and the very structure of the activities themselves, together with the teacher, take on the role of the scaffolding expert.

Brown and Campione's classrooms are designed so that learners can 'mutually appropriate' beliefs, skills, and practices from the ebb and flow of activity in the classroom zone of proximal development. In constructing a zone of proximal development for a particular task the expert—foremost perhaps the teacher, but, as we have seen, other elements as well—incorporates learners' actions into the expert's own system of activity.

> The fact that any action can always have more than one analysis makes cognitive change possible. Children can participate in an activity that is more complex than they can understand, producing 'performance before competence,' to use Cazden's (1981) phrase. While in the [zone of proximal development] of the activity, the children's actions get interpreted within the system being constructed with the teacher. Thus the child is exposed to the teacher's understanding without necessarily being directly taught (Newman et al. 1989: 63–64. cited in Brown et al. 1993: 193).

The core participant structures in Brown and Campione's classrooms are essentially collaborative and dialogical because:

> Dialogues provide the format for novices to adopt the discourse structure, goals, values, and belief systems of scientific practice. Over time, the community of learners adopts a common voice and common knowledge base . . . , a shared system of meanings, beliefs, and activity that is as often implicit as it is explicit (Brown et al. 1993: 194).

Brown and Campione's classrooms put a premium on social learning and discovery (and thus look 'progressive' and 'learner-centered'), but they do not advocate 'untrammelled discovery learning' (206). Although teacher and students together constitute a learning community, 'it is clearly the case that the adult teacher is first among equals, for she has a clear instructional goal' (205):

> In many forms of cooperative learning, students are left to construct learning goals for themselves; the goals change over time as interests

change, and groups sometimes concoct goals far different from those envisaged by the authorities. In our classroom, the research direction of the group is not so democratic.

Teachers are encouraged to hold goals for each research group, hoping that the students will reach those goals through their own efforts. But if they do not, the teacher will invite the students to arrive at a mature understanding by whatever means she can, including, as a last resort, explicit instruction . . .

Although there is considerable evidence that didactic teaching leads to passive learning, by the same token unguided discovery can be dangerous too. Children 'discovering' in our biology classrooms are quite adept at inventing scientific misconceptions. Teachers are encouraged to see these common problems as fruitful errors, way stages on the route to mature understanding that they can manipulate and direct in useful ways (Brown et al. 1993: 205–06).

Vygotsky's notion of a zone of proximal development, and the focus on social cognition, collaboration, and dialogue, are often associated with 'liberal' pedagogical theories and explicitly opposed to 'conservative' or 'traditional' ones. But with Brown and Campione's work we see how they can also be used as devices to 'manipulate' people (if we can use the term, for the time being, neutrally) into accepting, trusting, and committing themselves to the goals and values (the vision) of the leader (teacher) and the organizational system (technologies and activities) within which she operates.

Now back to the core dilemma of the new capitalism: how to control empowered units without a central authority. Brown and Campione's classrooms are a way station towards a system in which core values and goals are 'seeded' into social practices, activity systems, technologies, and flexible roles of the participants, as well as into the vision of non-authoritarian leaders (coaches), to be internalized as part and parcel of one's very participation in (and even co-construction of) the overall system. These core values and goals need not be visibly connected to or associated with any central controlling authority, nor need they ever be directly negotiated over in any very overt fashion. In Brown and Campione's classrooms, in fact, the 'real' source of goals and values is not the teacher, but the invisible cognitive scientists who have seeded the whole system with goals, values, and 'knowledge structures' to be 'mutually appropriated'.

What we are talking about here, in the end, is the way in which immersion into a 'community of practice' can allow individuals or units to internalize values and goals—often without a great deal of negotiation or conscious reflection and without the exercise of very much top-down authority. (See Bauman 1995: 275ff for a discussion of the dangers of the recent tendency in the social sciences to romanticize 'communities'.) Since this sort of approach offers an attractive solution to the core dilemma of the new capitalism, it is not surprising that we find appeals to it more and more often in the new-capitalist literature:

> The Institute for Research on Learning, a spinoff from Xerox's Palo Alto Research Center, is almost alone in studying the emergence and power of such knowledge-development activities. The center's particularly felicitous term is 'communities of practice,' as it is used by, for instance, IRL's Susan Stucky. 'Learning,' she says, 'is the process of becoming a member of a community of practice. The motivation to learn is the motivation to become a member.'
>
> Becoming a member of a community of practice is literally a requirement of modern-day job success (Peters 1994: 174).

Peters, a leading new-capitalist guru, is wrong in saying that IRL is almost alone—a whole bevy of cognitive scientists and educators engage in similar work (see e.g. Lave & Wenger 1991; Rogoff 1990). And, as we have seen, Brown and Campione, among others, have implemented such communities of practice in elementary school class-rooms. In fact, the concept of becoming a member of a community of practice has, in one guise or another, played a major role in much work on critical literacy, sociocultural literacy, collaborative and cooperative education, and 'distributed cognition', some of which is written from a radical political stance at some variance with new-capitalist texts (e.g. Bizzell 1992; Bloome & Green 1991; Edwards & Mercer 1987; Gee 1996).

In the end, then, we would argue that, given the core dilemma of the new capitalism, such notions as communities of practice, learning communities, and mutual appropriation of thought, beliefs, skills, and practices from a rich flow of activity in a zone of proximal development are central themes around which cognitive science and the new capitalism will align to their mutual benefit.

Note: we are not damning communities of practice here, nor are we downplaying the active and important role of teachers in such communities. In fact, as Chapter 1 makes clear, we believe that language, literacy, and learning are always and everywhere embedded in practice and socially and culturally distributed. We intend here only to point to the fact that such notions must be examined closely for the role they play in specific contexts and within the wider frames of social, political, and economic change. And we want to elicit open discussion of the goals and core values of schools and schooling.

IV A further note on practice

In communities of practice, whether in classrooms or new-capitalist workplaces, people develop 'tacit knowledge' (Nonaka and Takeuchi 1995). In fact, this is just the sort of knowledge in and of practice that allows workers to add value to the enterprise and to continually re-create communities of practice that can apprentice new workers through immersion. Tacit knowledge is not stateable, but learnable only through immersion in communities of practice. Such tacit knowledge is the true added value of the new knowledge-based work order, part of the core competencies that certain modern businesses actually include in their audits. Unfortunately for these businesses, the workers/partners own and can walk away with such tacit knowledge that has been built up in practice. This is, in fact, a major problem in the new capitalism. Empowered knowledge workers can take their knowledge and sell it to the highest bidder—indeed, fast capitalist texts, in stressing that all workers ought to be entrepreneurs, implicitly encourage this.

The underlying premise of the new work systems, then, is that every successful worker builds up knowledge about his or her job that is derived in part from participation in a community of practice, and in part from his or her own unique insights. The trick for business is how to capture this knowledge in a way that makes it increasingly accessible to other people in the organization, and how to retain it when workers walk away.

The solution here is this: distribute the knowledge across people and technology in such a way that no individual has any large part of it alone but, rather, each person functions as part and parcel of a 'knowledge system' (Nonaka & Takeuchi 1995; O'Connor 1993). This distributed system, made up of people and technology into which a lot of knowledge is offloaded, will adapt and change rapidly as a system. But it cannot be harmed by the loss of any one individual. Thus we can predict, we believe, that the new capitalism will focus more and more—as it already is beginning to do—on *sociotechnical practices*, not on people. And this is true, despite the fact that the popular literature of the new capitalism always celebrates the trusting and empowering of people. Thus, we see that distributed systems are, for the new capitalism, 'good business' in a great many respects.

The new capitalism, then, makes full contact with sociocultural theories of language, learning, and literacy, theories of the sort that in one guise underpin the work of people like Brown and Campione; theories that are very close to our own hearts, as all three of us have worked to help develop them. Both the new capitalism and sociocultural theory alike disown the idea of knowledge and learning as locked into and 'owned' by private minds. They both—for different reasons—argue that knowledge and learning are social and distributed across people and technology—beyond individual minds and bodies.

But the connections between the new capitalism and sociocultural theories run deeper yet: both of them—again for different reasons—advocate school reform centered on collaborative learning with a stress on communication skills. Collaboration and communication are the essential ingredients of work groups in which knowledge is distributed and embedded in the practice and not in the person. Furthermore, the new capitalism and sociocultural theory both put emphasis on *semiotics*, the ability to design, analyze, and transform symbols and symbolic value in social settings. After all, symbols, not commodities, are what the new capitalism has to sell, and what ultimately it wants its workers to produce.

Those of us who engage in sociocultural approaches to language and literacy are very much in the right place at the right time. But, as our ideas become cooptable within the new capitalism, we must focus clearly on where we differ from new-capitalist expressions of these ideas. First, as educators we must ensure, we believe, that all students come to understand the formation of social identities and the nature of social practices in their full cultural and historical contexts. By so widening the frame we allow our students to understand the complex systems of the new world in a deeper sense than the new capitalism might care to endorse.

Second, we differ from the new capitalism less now in our core ideas and tools than in our purposes, values, and politics. We must put these on the front burner in our conversations and in our work with students. In particular, as we discussed in the last chapter, when we broaden our framework to include the 'four-fifths' who are being impoverished by the new capitalism, we immediately come to acute political and moral issues that quickly transcend 'business vision' and 'worker empowerment' as sources of social amelioration.

As the distinction between 'learning' and 'doing' collapses in the contemporary work world, thanks to the knowledge and information explosion and to new technologies, we need to ask where the space for reflection and critique apart from immersion in the core values and communities of practice of the business will exist. Indeed, we need to reinvigorate the whole discussion of what constitutes reflection and critique—a 'critical literacy'—in our 'new times'.

V The new capitalism and the critics of capitalism

We turn now to our second and briefer story, the story of the new capitalism and those who would be its critics. The new capitalism is doublesided: talk of worker/partner empowerment sits side by side with calls for the appropriation of the core values of a visionary leader, a corporate system, or the new capitalism itself. Capitalism—of any form—has never been without its many critics.

There are, however, troubles in attempting to lodge traditional critiques of the new capitalism. The problem is this: the new capitalism has itself coopted a good deal of the language and many of the themes of ostensibly opposing movements. Take, for instance, the sorts of radical post-structuralist and postmodernist movements often associated by those who disdain them with the label 'political correctness'. The new capitalism blatantly blurs traditional identities (e.g. between 'workers' and 'managers'; 'products' and 'services'; 'practice/production' and 'knowledge'; it celebrates change and the absence of borders (e.g. breaking down the barriers between different units in a company or between different sorts of workers); and it encourages the undermining of overt authority (e.g. the undermining of hierarchies and direct control by 'bosses').

In these respects, as well as others, the new capitalism pre-empts radical postmodern themes and attitudes. Postmodern critics of capitalism, and of Western patriarchal imperialism in general, equally celebrate the dissolving of essences and identities, the absence and crossing of borders and divisions, and the undermining of control and authority. (There is a massive literature on postmodernism; see Best and Kellner 1991 for an overview.)

Since it would take us too far afield to fully develop the themes common to the new capitalism and postmodern theories, let us give a single example. One image that has played a major role in the literature on postmodernism is Bakhtin's image of 'carnival', conveyed in his book *Rabelais and His World*. Although carnivals are now minor events they played a major role in the Renaissance for all classes of people, and they were one of the few cultural spaces that evaded the direct control of the Roman Catholic Church. Let's listen to Katerina Clark and Michael Holquist (1984) talk about Bakhtin's ideas about 'carnival':

> Unlike ritual, carnival is not organized by a separate caste of specialists who create it according to their exclusive dictates, whether religious or aesthetic. Everybody makes carnival, everyone is carnival: 'Carnival is not a spectacle seen by the people; they live in it, and everyone participates because its very idea embraces all people.' Carnival extends a kind of general hegemony not only over everyone but also everywhere: 'While carnival lasts, there is no other life outside it. During carnival time life is subject only to its laws . . . the laws of freedom' [Bakhtin 1984: 7]. Carnival is a minimally ritualized antiritual, a festive celebration of the other, the gaps and holes in all mappings of the world laid out in systematic theologies, legal codes, normative poetics, and class hierarchies.
>
> Carnival must not be confused with mere holiday. The ability to revel in the world's variety, to celebrate its openness and its ever-renewed capacity to surprise, is a 'special form of life . . . ,' a kind of existential heteroglossia [Bakhtin 1984: 8]. Carnival is a gap in the fabric of society. And since the dominant ideology seeks to author the social order as a unified text, fixed, complete, and forever, carnival is a threat.
>
> The festive laughter engendered by carnival keeps alive a sense of variety and change. Such an emphasis on change and becoming is directly opposed to the official emphasis on the past, to a stasis so complete that it becomes eternity. Through carnival, the folk are 'freed from the oppression of such gloomy categories as "eternal", "immovable", "absolute", "unchangeable", and instead are exposed to the gay and free laughing aspect of the world, with its unfinished and open character, with the joy of change and renewal' [Bakhtin 1984: 81, 83] (Clark and Holquist 1984: 300–01; footnotes removed and replaced by references).

These sorts of themes are by now well known; they signal major motifs of postmodernism in its unsettling of such notions as 'authorship', 'unified texts', and 'single interpretations', and of the hegemonic sources of power that seek to uphold all of these. This is, however, hardly the kind of material we would have thought appealing to management consultants and capitalists in general. But Tom Peters, in his book *Liberation Management* (1992), picks just the image of carnival to characterize the emerging world of the new capitalism—and Peters, we would think, has never heard of Bakhtin. Peters argues that the current pace of change and the emphasis on customizing products and services to individual customers constitutes 'a clarion call for new imagery':

> In short, today's organizational images stink. Not just those that derive from the military ('Kick ass and take names') and 'pyramids' (heavy, steep, immobile), but even the new 'network', 'spiderweb', 'Calder mobile'. These modern notions are a mighty step forward, but they still miss the core idea of tomorrow's surviving corporation: dynamism.
>
> How about company-as-carnival? . . . Say 'carnival' and you think energy, surprise, buzz, fun. The mark of the carnival—and what makes it most different from a day at most offices—is its dynamism. Dynamism is its signature, the reason we go back. To create and maintain a carnival is never to get an inch away from dynamic imagery. As chief, you must feel the dynamics in your fingertips, be guided by them in *every* decision . . .
>
> The practical point for the firm's leaders: Constantly using dynamic imagery, thinking of yourself as running a carnival, and stomping out all forms of static thinking and imagery will help you toward the right structure and strategy for these woozy times.
>
> To wit: If you don't feel crazy, you're not in touch with the times! The point is vital. These are nutty times. Nutty organizations, nutty people, capable of dealing with the fast, fleeting, fickle, are a requisite for survival . . . (Peters 1992: 15–18).

Peters has no more use for the 'practical' and the 'utilitarian' than did Bakhtin or Renaissance peasants; he's as keen to smash hegemonies, unified hierarchical wholes, and standard practices, essences, and identities as is the most radical postmodernist. At Peters' carnival, however, it's as if the bishops and cardinals have shown up to smash the power of the Church: 'Change? Change! Yes, we've almost all, finally, embraced the notion that "change is the only constant." Well, sorry. Forget change! The word is feeble. Keep saying "revolution". (Peters 1994: 8).

Let us return briefly to Clark and Holquist's remarks on Bakhtin. The first paragraph resonates strongly with a number of major themes in the new-capitalist literature: the disdain for narrow specialists (as against understanding whole systems); the disavowal of hierarchical control ('exclusive dictates'); the emphasis on inclusion of everyone from workers to chief executives in the meaningful work and decisions of the business; and, perhaps most strikingly, the emphasis on the absence of life outside the carnival/business or, at least, the blurring of the boundaries between life inside and life outside. A passage in the same paragraph—'Carnival extends a kind of general hegemony not

only over everyone but also everywhere: "While carnival lasts, there
is no other life outside it. During carnival time life is subject only to
its laws . . . the laws of freedom" '—fits well with the new capitalism's '
colonization of private life and non-business spheres; as expressed in
Workplace 2000:

> In a *Harvard Business Review* article . . . David Kirp and Douglas
> Rice describe the expectations of these new hard-driving companies
> this way: 'What these "work hard, play hard" companies want is
> nothing less than total responsibility and over-the-edge loyalty.
> Employees are constantly on view and the line between work and
> play, the line between public and private becomes fuzzy' (Boyett
> and Conn 1992: 40).

To sum up this section we use an argument well developed by the
sociologist Zygmunt Bauman in his book *Intimations of Postmodernity* (1992). Bauman argues that as the world became 'modern' and
conditions became global the first response—the response of the 'old'
classical colonial and industrial capitalism—was to attempt to claim
universality and 'correctness' for Anglo Western culture and its
values—to colonize the rest of the world, to attempt to homogenize
other cultures in the image of the Western middle class. And it is this
response that the critics of capitalism are best poised to attack. But the
'new' post-industrial and post-colonial capitalism has found *virtue* in
diversity. Bauman puts the matter as follows:

> Contrary to the anguished forebodings of the 'mass culture' critics
> of the 1950s, the market proved to be the arch-enemy of uniformity.
> The market thrives on variety; so does consumer freedom and with
> it the security of the system. The market has nothing to gain from
> those things the rigid and repressive social system of 'classical'
> capitalism promoted: strict and universal *rules*, unambiguous criteria
> of *truth*, *morality and beauty*, indivisible *authority of judgement.*
> But if the market does not need those things, neither does the
> system. The powers-that-be lost, so to speak, all interest in
> universally binding standards (Bauman 1992: 52).

Our point is not that the language of the new capitalism and that
of postmodern and critical theories *mean* the same thing. Rather, it is
this: When non-authoritarian distributed systems come to the fore, in
classrooms, workplaces, governments, communities, and our lives,
much of the language and many of the themes of the traditional critique
of capitalism—based as it was and is on the critique of centralized
power and hierarchical systems—are coopted. In such a setting

capitalism—in its new capitalist form—can align itself, at least super-
ficially, with traditional *critics* of capitalism and Western hegemony.

It has not been our purpose here to offer a critique of the new
capitalism. We touched on such a critique in the previous chapter.
Instead, it has been our purpose to develop a better understanding of
new worlds and new alignments. It has also been our purpose to suggest
the need for renewed vigorous discussion of the *goals* of schooling,
society and life, as well as the creation of new languages of critical
engagement with the new capitalism. With this theoretical grounding
in place we are in a better position to see how it all pans out at
significant points in the real world.

4   A tale of one factory: training for teams

Fast capitalist texts of the sort we discussed in Chapter 2 are not usually based on sustained research in actual workplaces. Rather, their arguments are bolstered by anecdotes and apocryphal tales—uncritical accounts of particular corporations that have been transformed, of individual workers who have been empowered. These 'parables' play an important role in the rhetoric of the new capitalism, suggesting the outlines of the enchanted workplaces to which we should increasingly look forward, highlighting the effects of the differences between new forms of work and the old.

One such story, often repeated in the popular literature, features the jointly owned and managed US and Japanese automobile factory, NUMI, or New United Motors Inc., located in Milpitas, California. According to the story, one NUMI worker, after experiencing his company's reorganization into work teams and other 'high performance' innovations, took great pride and ownership in the work he did, in contrast to the demoralized, embittered attitudes of workers before the plant was restructured. This pride manifested itself, the story goes, when on a weekend outing with his family the worker spotted a new Geo automobile that he recognized as containing his own workmansl. p. Spontaneously, he wrote a note to leave on the windshield, revealing to the new owner that he had played a role in building the car, that he hoped the owner was enjoying it, and that should problems arise the owner should contact him personally. The story is meant to demonstrate a worker's attitude of ownership, responsibility, and pride, one that stands in sharp contrast to the feelings and activities of workers at the plant only months before when, after a protracted period of labor–management strife, absenteeism, and sabotage, the factory closed and its workers were laid off en masse.

Our point isn't to claim that such anecdotes have no basis in fact, but neither do we want to take such stories at face value as representative of the experiences of workers at NUMI or other new-capitalist workplaces. Rather, we want to call attention to the quite partial nature of the tale and argue that we need to investigate and understand, to document and analyze, the apparent successes along with the failures, struggles, negotiations, and compromises that characterize the reorganization of work in the new capitalist era. And we need to do so from as wide a variety of perspectives as possible, including those of workers, management, and labor.

While recognizing that any representation is necessarily partial, we argue for the need to draw portraits that are as complete a picture of the whole as possible, representations that don't evade complexities, contradictions or paradoxes. Fast capitalist texts aside, even the scholarly literature is short on long-term, first-hand studies of recent workplace change and innovation. Perhaps due to the difficulties inherent in gaining entry to workplaces as sites for research, perhaps due to the time- and labor-intensive nature of such research, most national and international scholarly conversations about the new capitalism take their arguments from survey and correlational data or from large-scale analyses of economic trends and developments. We are arguing here for the value of up-close, sustained looks at the experiences of people at their work. Only from such a vantage point will we be suitably equipped to hear and interpret stories such as the NUMI account. Furthermore, only from such a vantage point can we properly contextualise our more 'theoretical' discussion in Chapters 2 and 3.

As we have seen in the previous chapters, the rhetoric of fast capitalist texts emphasizes not only that a new work order is inevitable for companies that will remain competitive globally but that new forms of work, in many cases, also simultaneously converge with more humane, more satisfying, more intellectually fulfilling forms of work. Thus we hear how middle managers have disappeared, their roles and responsibilities passed on to front-line workers, who have become partners engaging in meaningful work, identifying and solving problems, actively seeking to improve their productivity and quality performance, continually increasing their own skills and the value they add to their company, often through educational programs provided at or sponsored through their workplace.

In essence, the new economic order carries with it the promise of a new moral order, which is all the more reason to look closely at the phenomena, to bring first-hand participant observation and ethnographic research to bear on the accounts provided in the popular literature, questioning how they measure up to the experiences of workers on the frontlines of economic change. We need to ask then, according to workers' lived experiences, in what ways are they empowered in new workplaces, and in what ways are traditional hierarchies and roles still in place? Or, framed within a sociocultural studies perspective, we want to determine what particular social identities workers are expected to construct and display, and what related social practices they are expected to learn, demonstrate, and value. What ways of talking, listening, reading, writing, acting, interacting, believing, and valuing are expected in newly organized and restructured workplaces, and how close or far are these from an egalitarian ideal of empowerment?

The following two chapters offer a case study that suggests what can be learned from sustained participant observation in workplaces and, indeed, the necessity of such research if we are to understand the nature and implications of the new capitalism as comprehensively and critically as we must. In constructing this case we have foregrounded the contradictions and paradoxes in the data, hoping thereby to build a representation that does justice to the complexity of people's lived experience.

Our case concerns an electronics assembly factory in the Silicon Valley of Northern California. At the beginning of the work reported here, the factory was in its second year of reorganization around self-directed work teams of a sort that embodied much of the popular rhetoric of fast capitalist texts. In this chapter we first offer a little background on the Silicon Valley and the electronics industry, as well as on the individual factory where the research was conducted. Then we provide an insider's view of the workings of teams at this factory: first by examining a training class where workers met to acquire the sensibilities and skills that the company believed they needed in order to operate in teams, and then—in the next chapter—by looking at a team meeting, where workers enacted their understanding of that curriculum and what the teams, and they as team members, could do and be.

I Background: from orchards to electronics

Riding south on Interstate 80 from Oakland, California, toward San José, the temperature and the scenery change. The deeper one goes into the Santa Clara Valley, and the farther away from San Francisco Bay, the hotter it gets. And although the Diablo Mountain Range is always in view in the distance, the immediate landscape is soon dominated by miles and miles of the sprawl of one-storey, modern, prosperous, cheerful-looking stucco buildings with names recognizable to those in the know in the computer industry: Intel, Sun, Flextronics, Hewlett-Packard, Lexitron, Apple, Silicon Graphics.

This is the famous Silicon Valley, and although one can find examples of industries other than electronics here (indeed, the NUMI automobile plant is located on I 80 just outside Milpitas) this twenty-five mile strip of the San Francisco peninsula belongs to the design and manufacture of computer boards, chips, and components. It is hard to believe that all these tracts of buildings and parking lots with some 2000 high-tech companies were, as late as the 1950s, orchards of apricots and walnuts.

The Silicon Valley region is often held up as a major economic success story in the United States. As is widely known, in the 1980s the country's manufacturing base downsized dramatically and also moved many of its operations overseas, putting many working people in the United States, who had, by and large, become accustomed to decent pay, out of work, and leaving those who kept their jobs accountable for more. The trend has continued in the 1990s, accompanied recently by the mandated shrinkage of the US military machine and the closure of military bases across the country, with California being especially hard hit.

In the midst of the turmoil and economic disarray created by these massive changes, the Silicon Valley has stood apart, growing steadily, even booming in the 1980s, keeping a significant proportion of its manufacturing at home, and even defeating, at last count, a Japanese challenge in chip production—and this despite a Statewide exodus of manufacturers who refused to cope with the State's environmental regulations and comparatively higher taxes and wages. It is no surprise, then, that companies in the Silicon Valley regularly play host to foreign dignitaries and US political figures who come to pay homage at this outpost of economic ingenuity.

This is not to say that the Valley hasn't experienced a share of economic difficulty. Almost totally dependent on the electronics industry, the area feels any drop in electronics sales or related economic downturns acutely. In the early 1990s, for example, many computer-related companies announced salary cuts, layoffs, and plant closings, including the largest layoff in Apple Computer's history. Other high-tech firms similarly downsized or moved their production facilities to other, less expensive areas of the State, and some left the State entirely. There have been investigations of and penalties for toxic leaks and air pollution. The jury is still out, then, as to how the Valley will weather the most recent economic turbulence, but early signs, such as a boom in the sales of multimedia electronics gear, the expanding infrastructure of the information superhighway, and the rapid expansion of the individual factories studied here, suggest that the Silicon Valley will most likely continue its economic wizardry.

There are various explanations for the Valley's development and success, including the availability of intellectual resources and support at local colleges and universities, as well as access to ready capital, including billions from the US federal government for research and development. But most accounts also acknowledge the role played by young entrepreneurs who plied their considerable technical knowhow and sharp business sense into multimillion dollar enterprises. These young entrepreneurs are said to have constructed, and been influenced by, a unique local industrial environment, where fierce competition operated within a collegial atmosphere of interfirm cooperation and networking.

Annalee Saxenian (1994), who has analyzed the nature of this environment and assessed the ways it has provided regional advantage in the United States, describes the Valley as a 'network-based industrial system that promotes collective learning and flexible adjustment'. Despite intense interfirm competition, she argues, companies learn informally from each other, communicating and collaborating as the need arises. Saxenian sees much to praise in these 'loosely linked team structures [which] encourage horizontal communication among firm divisions and with outside suppliers and customers' (2–3). Here, then, we see the themes of 'networking', 'distributed knowledge', and 'distributed systems' that we in the previous chapter argued were major motifs of the new capitalism.

What is missing from this picture is the front-line worker. It is important to note, we think, that conversations about the success and development of the Valley (and other such regions in the United States and beyond) usually take place with scant reference to 80 percent of its workforce, the men and women who manufacture silicon chips and assemble circuit boards, the people who do the actual work of production. What is often left out of such accounts is the extreme segmentation of the Valley's workforce—into highly skilled technical and professional workers, at the top, and the much more numerous production workers, often recent immigrants from Asia and Latin America who don't earn a lot more than the minimum wage and for whom opportunities to advance are few.

The case study to be presented here and in the next chapter will, by contrast, focus on Silicon Valley production workers, in particular workers at a circuitboard assembly plant. This factory performs contract work for big-name electronics companies such as Intel, Apple, and Silicon Graphics, but is well known in the Valley in its own right as a fast-growing, enormously successful company, head and shoulders above the competition. We want to situate the success of the Valley, its entrepreneurs, and one electronics factory within an account of the working lives of 'ordinary' employees—the newly empowered 'partners' or 'associates' of the new capitalism.

II More background: contract manufacturing

In recent years temporary work has become more and more prevalent— in fact, such jobs are the fastest growing category of job in the new capitalism. Temporary jobs provide workers with no job security and few benefits like health insurance, but enable corporations to adjust their labor overheads to the ebb and flow of the market (Parker 1994). Indeed, the largest employer in the United States is Manpower Inc., a temporary-employment agency.

A parallel and complementary phenomenon is contract manufacturing, also called 'outsourcing', and in fact contract manufacturers depend heavily on temporary workers. Contract manufacturers perform services for other companies, services that were once performed by the companies themselves. For example, while big computer companies like Apple and IBM used to assemble all their own circuit boards inhouse for their own products, it is now customary to farm out this aspect of their production. A recent report showed that over half of the 1000 electronics companies surveyed were using contract manufacturers, though they had not been doing so as recently as five years ago. Early on, during the 1960s, Silicon Valley firms drew on contract manufacturers to assemble their boards mainly in peak periods when demand was too great for the companies to handle themselves. These contract manufacturing houses were called 'board-stuffers'. They were small, marginal firms that paid immigrant workers, often women, very low wages to attach components to boards by hand. Workers labored in sweatshops or took the work home. The components and materials were provided by the customer along with design instructions and directions for assembly. In essence, all the contract manufacturers provided was bodies. There are still board-stuffing houses in the Valley, although many of these shops have moved to Asia and Latin America where wages are even cheaper.

Contract manufacturing in circuit board assembly has changed a lot since the heyday of board-stuffing. In the 1980s big companies like Sun, IBM, and Hewlett-Packard started to rely on contract manufacturers to do more of their work so that they could further reduce their costs, have a quicker turnaround time for their products, or focus themselves on other aspects of manufacturing such as product development.

Simultaneously, and also as a result of an increase in business, circuit board companies began to invest in expensive new technologies, in particular, robot-controlled surface-mounting techniques. In the past, boards had been assembled mainly by hand using what was called 'through-hole' technology; that is, workers soldered individual leads from an integrated circuit through the holes in the boards. Surface-mounting techniques, on the other hand, use epoxy to glue tiny electronic components onto both sides of the boards. This technology is much more complicated and capital-intensive than through-hole is. It is described as five to ten times harder to process, and just one line of surface-mounting robots costs over a million dollars.

Computer firms were happy to let contract manufacturers invest in this costly technology (contractors could turn a profit despite the required investments in technology given their high volume) and to gradually turn over more and more of their assembly work to them. As the companies developed relationships over time and built up trust in each other, the firms began to depend on contract houses for more sophisticated services, such as board design and testing and the procurement of components. And thus the shape and significance of contract manufacturing changed radically over the years.

The dark side of this development is that, in relying on contractors, electronics companies no longer have to make commitments to many people, who were once their workers, in terms of job security or health plans or decent wages (Siegel 1993). And as it is customary among circuit board assembly plants in the Valley to rely heavily on temporary workers, wages are low (from eight to ten dollars an hour) and layoffs and enforced overtime—depending on the vagaries of customer demand—are the norm. None of these Silicon Valley factories is unionized.

Being a contract manufacturer has particular implications for doing business and, as we shall see, implications as well for the skills its workforce is called upon to develop and use, especially literacy. A company chooses one contract manufacturer over another because of lower costs, high quality, and productivity, so there is much ado in these companies about minimizing defects and speeding up production.

Because technology changes so quickly these days a contract manufacturer's customers can be expected to be particularly demanding, calling for changes in boards that are already in production and regularly returning old boards to be reworked and updated at short notice. Record-keeping on these occasions is paramount; customers want to know what changes were made on which boards on what dates and by whom. Paper trails are thick.

Customers also want to be assured of a certain level of competence before they bring their business, and thus circuit board assemblers, like a growing number of other US and European firms, vie to be certified by international standards agencies (see *Fortune Magazine*, 28 June 1993). These agencies enforce stringent procedures concerning documentation, so that factories are practically afloat in a sea of paper. It is customary for every single procedure that takes place within such a certified factory to be written down and documented. Workers' activities and practices are expected to match the printed account and are regularly audited to ensure that they do so.

This history of the Valley and contract manufacturing raises many questions when we consider it in light of recent attempts to build high-performance work organizations around self-directed work teams. Such teams—and the whole concept of collaboration and 'communities of practice'—are key ingredients of new-capitalist workplaces, and come highly recommended in the fast-capitalist literature.

The idea of self-directed work teams raises a variety of questions. Given that most production workers in the Valley are poorly compensated and overworked now, how will they respond to requirements that they develop new work practices that depend on the development of new work-related skills, such as collaboration, goal-setting, and new forms of literacy? How will they greet increased work demands, such as perpetual training, reams of required documentation and data analysis, and ever spiralling quality and productivity goals? How will managers and supervisors, many of whom are white and all of whom necessarily deal with a multicultural, multilingual workforce, respond to their charge to create a new work 'culture'? How will they envision instruction and training, and what attitudes will they bring to the table about their employees' abilities and motivations? How will they manage changes in their own responsibilities, some of which they will be expected to hand over to the front-line workforce?

In sum, in these changing situations, what new social identities will people construct? To begin addressing some of these questions we turn to our case study of 'Teamco', a pseudonym chosen to highlight this company's recent investment in teams.

III A note on methods

The case study reported here is part of a larger project directed by Glynda Hull and designed to compare the skill requirements of traditionally organized workplaces with those of high performance workplaces. (The original research was funded by the US National Center for Research in Vocational Education and the National Center for Research in Writing and Literacy.) At the time this book was written, Hull and her team had spent one year at Teamco, and three years in total at circuit board assembly factories in Silicon Valley. Ethnographic methods were used for data collection, most commonly observations and interviews, many of which were audiotaped or videotaped.

The research team also participated in the work of the factories on occasion, assembling the simpler products or helping out with literacy-related duties. One long afternoon, for instance, was spent with the lead worker of one of the 'handload' lines, meticulously combing the files of each set of manufacturing process instructions for each assembly in the plant. The task was to determine the exact number of components that workers were expected to load for each assembly, figures that would then be plugged into a new formula for determining 'standard times' or how fast people would need to work. This task, like many other new responsibilities for the workers, grew from the company's interest in making teams accountable for improving productivity.

Hull's public and official role in the factory was as 'researcher', leading a group from a local university in studying the company's attempt to reorganize itself around self-directed work teams. The researchers attended the initial training program provided to induct workers into teams, and then, over several months, attended the meetings of those teams. In the latter context the researchers were at times called upon to help out, in the role of teachers rather than co-workers. The assistance provided often had to do with literacy issues—for example, teaching team members to read graphs, use computer programs, and apply mathematical formulae.

In one other way, as well, the researchers' role in the factory went beyond the usual notions of 'participant observation', and crisscrossed the boundaries traditionally (and artificially) set between the researcher and the researched. The researchers frequently provided some personal assistance to individuals. Since many workers were recent immigrants whose English was shaky, researchers were regularly relied upon as language intermediaries. Once a worker who moonlighted in a Chinese restaurant brought in the menu so that a researcher could record the English pronunciation of 'pot stickers' and 'vegetable fried rice.' Researchers intervened on many occasions for a young supervisor, an ethnic Chinese who grew up in Vietnam but had developed an American penchant for credit cards and mail order houses. Her query 'What is sweepstake?', began a months' long saga of negotiations with a disreputable mail order house over $899 worth of pens. Researchers read and commented upon essays from night school, interpreted traffic tickets and insurance policies, ventured opinions regarding medical options, and exchanged business cards with anxious parents happy to know a professor from the university at which their sons or daughters were enrolled or had aspirations of attending.

The researchers' roles as language and cultural brokers helped build trust between the researchers and people from whom they were separated by a vast cultural and social gulf. These relationships helped immeasurably as the researchers attempted to understand work activities and social positions on the shop floor. The goal was to understand workers by placing them within their historical, social, cultural and work contexts as fully as possible. In the same way, then, that a factory can usefully be understood as the product of multiple influences—its industry, its local history, the current economic climate, the vision of its managers—so can the attitudes, abilities, and actions of workers be usefully interpreted in light of their work and educational backgrounds, their individual styles and creativities, their cultures and genders.

IV Teamco: contract manufacturer par excellence

Three flags mark the entrance to the Teamco 'campus': the US Stars and Stripes, the California State bear, and the Teamco emblem, which looks something like a starburst or an electrical storm. Even if you didn't know that the company was successful—a force in the industry to be reckoned with and a business institution quite conscious of its public image—you would very likely reach such a conclusion by touring the San José plant: building after building, large and low, gleaming white in the sun, flanked by parking lots filled to bursting, everything neat, shiny, and clean, and everywhere hundreds of Asian workers and other people of color, busy, intent, and purposeful.

The research team first learned about Teamco by reading trade journals, mostly articles describing its rapid success and its management strategies, and continued to monitor the journals as the study progressed. The story of Teamco reads not unlike the entrepreneurial success stories of other Silicon Valley companies with similarly humble beginnings. In the unique regional culture of Silicon Valley, the story goes, visionary men were able to parlay an ingenuous business sense and a willingness to work hard into an electronics empire, and that empire bred other visionaries who eventually formed their own companies. And so Teamco was founded in the late 1970s by an executive with management experience gleaned from a major computer company. It began as a small repair house for certain types of printers but moved quickly into circuit board assembly. Its sales increased twentyfold in ten years and in 1994 the company reached a sales figure of well over a billion dollars. Teamco is now touted as one of the 'hottest' manufacturers in the Silicon Valley, the recipient of scores of customer awards and national and international recognition.

Accounts of Teamco's success in the 1980s pay homage to its adherence to Japanese-style management strategies, and indeed the company's president is said to have made several trips to Japan to study their techniques at first hand. Kaizen (continuous improvement), the Five Ss (Japanese words beginning with 's' for orderliness, cleanliness, discipline, etc.), poka-yoke (mistake-proofing the process). Name a quality enhancement approach—Teamco executives have been glad to try it.

More recent accounts of the company highlight its investment in its multicultural workforce. First came Teamco Tech, an inhouse university, which offered courses not only in basic electronics and statistical process control but in English-as-a-Second-Language and American Culture. The impetus for this venture is said to have been management's desire to improve communication, since its workers speak some 15 different languages and 40 dialects.

Then, three years ago, Teamco's current self-improvement initiative began—the organization of the factory around self-directed work teams (SDWTs). These were the brainchild of a manager in charge of strategic development. The effort involved first a series of seminars for middle and upper managers, to introduce the need for a site-wide reorganization around teams and the reduction of management layers. The next step was to create a curriculum and training program for non-exempt or hourly workers, and to put 3000 workers through some 50 hours of training. In conjunction with the training, or after its completion, workers were divided into approximately 200 SDWTs which corresponded to their work areas.

The most recent phase of the project has been the linkage of compensation to team performance—determined by whether individual teams have been able to meet their productivity and quality goals for the quarter. There is also a system in place to reward individual teams who compete against each other at company-wide forums and are judged on their presentation and their problem-solving. The research team observed the training, sat in on meetings and competitions of a range of teams, and has followed the progress of these teams from their beginning.

As in the quality enhancement programs started earlier at Teamco, the impetus for self-directed work teams seems to have been a corporate desire, similarly espoused by most of today's *Fortune* 500 companies, to continue to improve, to embrace change as inevitable, to try whatever might work in a never-ending, all-consuming quest to remain competitive in a cut-throat marketplace. Whatever could be done to better serve the company's customers—that is, to increase productivity and to reduce the incidence of quality flaws—should be done. Although Teamco's past management strategies for increasing its market share and its profits had certainly paid off handsomely, the company came to think that what had worked in the past couldn't be trusted to work in the future, and that they would be foolish to rest on their laurels. And so began what various Teamco executives and trainers have referred to as a 'culture change', the introduction of a whole new way of thinking, acting, and being for workers and managers both. Here we see up close the makings of new social identities (new 'kinds of people') through new social practices embedded in new and dynamically changing workplace Discourses.

This change was billed by most as a major shift, despite the company's past history of embracing quality enhancement programs. For one thing, organization of the company around self-directed work teams required all of the different divisional units of Teamco to play the same music, to read from the same page, rather than to operate autonomously. In the past, each division of Teamco had acted virtually like its own little company, with little interference or help from upper management, so long as they turned the expected profit. That would come to an end, now, as workers in all divisions experienced the same SDWT curriculum and as the company oversaw each team's performance by measuring their achievement of team goals and compared that performance across divisions.

A second challenge to reorganization around teams was the company's diverse workforce, with its myriad languages and cultures. Teamco had long been known as an 'Asian' company, though this term falsely implies a homogeneity that does not exist among people from many different Asian cultures. (One of the present authors JPG, who was born in San José, remembers that in the 1960s, the electronic assembly plants were staffed almost entirely by local Mexican-American women, i.e. Chicanas. Visiting the plant, after many years away from San José, the nature of 'global' change and its rearrangement of the 'local' was brought most powerfully home to him.) In recent years Teamco had also begun to hire non-Asian-American workers; it is said that the impetus for this change was becoming a public company and worries about lawsuits regarding discrimination. Many workers were then, and still are, recent immigrants, and since their English skills are still developing they speak to each other in Chinese or Vietnamese or Spanish on the shop floor, and tend to associate mostly with members of their own cultural groups. Such linguistic practices are workable, company executives reasoned, as long as divisions operate autonomously. But once a company culture calls for collaboration, for cross-divisional communication, indeed for teamwork, then there is a need for a common language, English, and a shared workplace culture that crosses ethnic boundaries.

Finally, we should note that the company's reliance on a largely temporary workforce also seemed certain to affect its effort to bring about a culture change. In fact, the company practice is to hire no employees directly; everyone is brought in as a temporary employee through a local agency. At times, as many as half of the factory's non-exempt or hourly employees have been temporaries. Whether these employees were made permanent (and then received benefits like health insurance), and when they were made permanent, depended on the vagaries of business, of customer demand. This hiring practice, of course, has ramifications in relation to training—the official policy at Teamco is that workers must be made permanent before they can attend SDWT classes, though practice on this point has varied—and one would think that it would have an impact as well on workers' commitment to their company's culture change.

V A training class

Perhaps the best place to go to get a sense of the cultural change initiated at Teamco is the training room, where the workers went to be introduced to the notion of SDWTs and to begin acquiring the skills they would need in functioning as teams. This is one crucial site in the ongoing creation of the new capitalist Discourse and its new 'kinds of people'. As always, however, a new Discourse arises in dynamic and complex interactions with older Discourses and other identities.

The curriculum of an educational program presumably embodies the core values of a Discourse and thus offers us a chance to understand key assumptions about learners, knowledge, and identity. Teamco's SDWT training program ought, then, to reveal the new roles that workers were expected to construct, the new identities or ways of thinking, acting, talking, and valuing that they were expected to take on. We start with a brief overview of the curriculum and its organization, to be followed by a detailed description and analysis of one classroom session.

The training classes at Teamco took place in a well-lit, high-ceilinged room that was cool, clean, and well appointed with black metal, cushioned chairs and several rows of gray formica tables configured like the letter E. Two of the walls were floor-to-ceiling plate glass windows covered by light gray blinds. In the front of the room were a television set with a VCR mounted on a cart, a dry-erase board, an easel, an overhead projector, and a 10 by 12 foot high-quality projection screen. Along the fourth wall, placed well above eye level, were a series of posters articulating Teamco's SDWT philosophy, including the definition and goals of self-directed work teams. Overall, the room had a modern, high-tech feel, and to those accustomed to the aging infrastructure and scant resources of public schools it appeared very inviting.

During classes there were approximately 15 to 25 front-line employees present. In the classes observed there was an even mix of women and men; nearly all were Asian-American, about 80 percent Vietnamese, with a sprinkling of other ethnicities, including Chinese, Filipino, Mexican, and Puerto Rican. All these workers spoke languages other than English as their first language, and many were bilingual or trilingual, speaking, for example, Vietnamese, Mandarin, and English, or Tagalog and English, or Spanish and English.

Some workers were quite proficient in English, as was Juan, who will be introduced below, but others had grave difficulties in understanding lectures and reading materials and participating in classes, which were carried out in their entirety in English by official policy. Interestingly, in the recent past Teamco had conducted at least some parts of its quality enhancement programs in four different languages— posters and other literature were written in English, Spanish, Chinese, and Vietnamese.

But the SDWT effort would be in English only. 'We consciously made the decision that we would not ESL this program', explained one member of the training department. The rationale was that, first of all, given the structure provided by a team, people who knew the language could help those who didn't, and thereby excellent workers who were poor communicators in English could still participate and contribute. This sharing of skill, by the way, as we saw in Chapter 3, is also the rationale behind such educational methods in school reform as 'reciprocal teaching' and other collaborative methods that render individuals' knowledge and skills public and distribute them across group members.

As far as the classes went, according to this trainer, the company wasn't overly concerned that workers absorbed every little detail of the curriculum: 'Understanding the material is not really our goal. The goal is for the team to understand why they're a team and the fact that they have certain specific goals. They're given the power to solve their own problems and to improve their own productivity.'

So it seems that the major purpose of the classes was to inculcate new attitudes and a new sensibility toward work, a process that was assumed not to depend on perfect English. Later, as workers actually took part in team meetings, they would acquire the needed knowledge and skills through immersion in real work activities and through collaborating with fellow team members. Here again we see the principle of immersion in a community of practice as a key theme of the new capitalism, just as it is in many school reform efforts of the sort we discussed in Chapter 3.

At the outset of training each worker was supplied with an inhouse textbook, a smart-looking three-ring binder with tabbed sections for some fifteen different topics, including Effective Team Meetings, Basic Finance, Problem-Solving Skills, Understanding Differences, Effective Listening, Handling Problems, and Accepting Change. Note here, even in the topics, we see the blurring between 'public' and 'private', the

Discourse boundary-crossing, and the colonization of the lifeworld so typical of the new capitalism.

Each chapter contained a list of learning objectives, a series of exercises (some to be done individually, some in groups), and a section for employees to record what they had learned each day. According to Teamco's training department, most of the curriculum was standard fare, available from vendors who specialize in corporate quality enhancement programs—'everything is out there', as one trainer put it. These materials were simply collected and customized and repackaged in the context of this company's interest in teams. (Indeed, we've come across some of the same exercises, such as how to construct a 'fishbone' diagram of the potential causes of a manufacturing problem, in the training literature of other companies.)

To give a sense of the curriculum, the ideas it embodies about teams, and the new identities suggested for workers through the enactment of that curriculum, we will shortly present portions of a transcript from a class meeting (Lesson 10 Accepting Change). As you go through the material it will be useful if you monitor what is happening in the class and how. What ideas are workers acquiring about work, in this case, about accepting change at work, and how will these ideas affect their expectations about teams and their roles as team members? What pedagogy is in place here—how does the class operate, and what does it require of participants? And what implications does the teaching approach have for workers' burgeoning identities as members of self-directed work teams, a core 'role' or 'identity' within the larger new-capitalist worker (partner) Discourse?

Gladis, the instructor, had been at Teamco for only a year, but was playing a very active role in SDWT training. At this point she had taken 300 workers through all 20 lessons in the curriculum, and she taught as many as eleven classes a week. In the class to be discussed Gladis was subbing for an absent teacher. Present in the class were Thanh, Juan, Aurelia, Tuyet, Phan, Kim, Nham, Niko, Lan, Khim Sa, Phong, Tam, Vuong, Hoang, and two researchers. Of these students only a few played parts in the class or figure at all in the transcript provided below. As we will see, there was very little 'class participation'. But let us briefly introduce three of these worker/students in order to give a sense of the range of their backgrounds and their attitudes towards teams.

> Juan told us that he was Puerto Rican (although the Spanish-speaking researcher among us suspected that he was Salvadorian, given his accent and vocabulary, and that for citizenship reasons he claimed the

other origin). Young, twenty-something, and very upbeat about his work, his schooling, and teams, Juan was a permanent employee. He had worked almost everywhere on the shop floor—in mechanical assembly (where large parts are affixed to circuit boards by hand or other products are assembled); in solder pot (where a worker holds a board over a fountain of molten solder and attaches one component at a time); in wave (where parts are glued to boards 'mechanically' and en masse as they pass through a large machine on a conveyor belt); in touch-up (where repairs and final touches are added by hand). Juan thought the electronics industry afforded him a lot of opportunity. He was proud of his on-the-job training, and showed the researchers his training certificates several times, along with his SDWT badge and stickers. A swing-shift worker, Juan took classes at a local community college during the day, where he was working toward an AS degree in electronics; he hoped this would lead eventually to an engineering degree or a managerial position at Teamco. He particularly looked up to Teamco's one Latino engineer, whom he viewed as a friend and mentor. Juan's English was quite good, and during SDWT classes he was often called on by the teacher to read; occasionally he would translate or speak for other Spanish background employees, such as Aurelia. On the last day of class, when the instructor asked for comments about teams, Juan said that teams were very important, and everyone ought to be on one. Later he became the leader of the team from the wave area.

Hoang, a Vietnamese-American also in his early twenties, worked on the touch-up line. He had been in the United States about one year and had recently been made a permanent employee at Teamco. Hoang had much trouble with English, although he told us he could understand more than he could express. He, too, was taking classes at a community college, ESL, but wasn't fond of his teacher who had told him not to participate. Also, he felt the ESL lessons there were too simple—just rote grammar and very little actual conversation. Hoang loved to sit and talk with the researchers during break time because he said it was one of the few occasions he had to speak English. And sometimes, even during work, as the researchers walked past his line, Hoang would swivel his chair around to converse with them, although workers down the line yelled to him in Vietnamese to get back to work—comments he let roll off his back. In SDWT classes Hoang was apt to joke and laugh at other people who were having trouble with English—a way of venting his own frustration, we would wager. However, he seemed to apply himself in class, reading along with the teacher, repeating words under his breath, writing down words that he didn't know, looking to the researchers for help. Hoang was not enamored of SDWT classes or the concept of teams. He summed up

his attitude toward classes by noting: 'I'm not a parrot'. Hoang quit
his job at Teamco after being employed there about 14 months; his
co-workers aren't sure where he went.

Aurelia was a friend of Hoang's; they sat next to each other in the
touch-up line and often talked and joked. Originally from Mexico,
Aurelia had been in the United States twelve years. In her late
twenties, she was married with two children. She was the only
non-Vietnamese worker on the line. Although Aurelia went through a
six-month course in electronics training, during which she learned to
read electronic color codes and to hand-solder, her work at Teamco
had been quite circumscribed. She started off in touch-up, snapping
components into sockets, and was now removing masking from boards
and performing similar mechanical tasks. According to another Latina
in the factory, this lack of mobility botherered Aurelia and was one
sign among many that the company discriminated against non-Asian
workers. But to the researchers Aurelia said that she liked her current
job, which she preferred to the more tedious hand-soldering:
'Sometimes easy, sometimes hard. But I like it, mechanical.' Although
her English was somewhat limited, Aurelia had made progress in the
year that the researchers knew her. Within the SDWT class she
worked hard to improve her English, focusing on the workbook and
following along as her teacher read, mouthing words she didn't know,
seeking help from the researchers. She reported that she liked the
classes because they gave her the chance to practise English, but that
she didn't learn much else: 'We don't learn nothing. Uh, I forgot it.
No, I forgot everything. But it's good because we learn more English.'

There were older workers at the factory, too, and workers who
represented a range of educational levels.

Before proceeding, we want to add a note here about reading the
transcripts. We have chosen to include some chunks of talk, with
summaries interspersed, in order to provide a realistic sense of what
the class was like by reproducing as best we can its language and
activities. In the following excerpts the numbers in square brackets
refer to the length of pauses in seconds; words in square brackets are
information provided by the researchers; empty parentheses represent
indecipherable speech; and filled parentheses indicate our best guess
at what was said.

Now to the class. Gladis the instructor began by making sure that
everyone had signed in; otherwise, she warned, they would have to
repeat the session. Then, as was customary, the class reviewed the last
week's lesson, which was Handling Problems. We pick up with
Gladis asking whether anyone remembers the steps involved in handling

problems. She then goes on to review the basic principles of self-directed work teams (printed on one of the company posters high on the wall), and from there she introduces the topic of the day, Accepting Change.

Gladis: 'Anybody remember the steps? [2] What are the steps to handling problems? [3] You can go back [1] to that lesson if you want to [almost 1] and take a look at the steps. [2] Somebody want to read 'em?' [4] Taking a volunteer. [3] Any volunteers?

Male: [to the fellow sitting next to him] You.

Several people: [laugh]

Gladis: You'd love to volunteer each other, huh?

Group: [laugh]

Gladis: Kim?

Kim: Yes [softly].

Gladis: Okay, thank you.

Kim: [reading from binder] Uhm, ( ) number one tell him of the problem as soon as possible. Number 2. Have facts when you are telling him about the problem. Number 3. Give him a chance to express his opinion. Number 4. Review the facts to ( ). Number 5. Discuss useful solution. Number 6. Decide what each of you will do to correct the problem.

Gladis: Okay, thank you Kim. Okay, six steps to handling problems. [3] Did anyone have an opportunity to use any of these steps to handling problems in this last week? [2] Anybody? Nobody had any problems this week?

Male: No.

Gladis: No?

Male: No.

Gladis: Okay. Well I guess that's, good. What about basic principles? Anybody have an opportunity to practise their basic principles? [3] No. [3] [Looking up at the Basic Principles poster on the wall] Nobody helped 'maintain someone's self-confidence or self-esteem'? [2] 'Maintain good relationships with your co-workers'? Bet you all did that. Right . . . Alright. The topic for today is going to be learning to accept change. Change is a fact of life. Alright. For a company like Teamco changes are constantly occurring. Alright. It's just a way the company wants to make an improvement,

> there's got to be constant change. A lot of times
> we don't like some of those changes. Uhm, we just
> have to learn how to deal with them. And this is
> why we're teaching you this class, so that you can
> learn those skills in learning to accept change in a
> positive way rather than a negative way.

At this point Gladis reads from her teacher's guide the distinction between 'changes we are in control of' and 'changes that are imposed on us'. The latter is the type the class will be learning about—when you get a new boss, she explains, or a work process has changed or you are asked to switch shifts or you have a reduction in work hours. She introduces the notion of change by reminding oldtimers, those who have been at Teamco for more than two years, that many changes have already taken place. She asks for examples of changes, but people don't respond, in part because only three employees fall into the oldtimer category.

After many questions and proddings, she creates a list of changes: the introduction of self-directed work teams; the color, length, and laundry requirements of the smocks that workers are required to wear (this is a change that Gladis brought up); new buildings; a new teacher (a reference to Gladis); new supervisors; new bosses. One worker tries to explain a change in the production line, but Gladis has trouble understanding her pronunciation, and twelve conversational turns are given to clarification, with Juan's assistance.

Next, the class reads a memo written in 1829 by the Governor of New York State to President Jackson complaining about the replacement of canal boats with trains. The text of this memo is set out in Figure 1.

After the class reads the memo silently, Gladis asks questions, much in the mode of a reading comprehension test. 'What changes did the Governor object to?' she wants to know, and eventually elicits responses that the Governor thought that trains travelled too fast and that women and children would be frightened by their speed. Someone also points out that the Governor objected to the expected loss of jobs among boat builders. Gladis then goes on to comment on how most people respond negatively to change, as did the Governor:

> *Gladis*: Alright, we do know that trains are our system of
> transportation, so it did happen even if he didn't
> want the change. He wrote to the President and he
> had to accept the change, but he was very negative

Figure 1: Memo to President Jackson from the Governor of New York

TO: President Jackson
FROM: Martin VanBuren Governor
DATE. January 31, 1829

The water canal boats of America are the most important kinds of transportation we know today. If we do not have canal boats, and have railroad trains, this would not be a good idea because:

1. Boat builders will lose jobs. The towline, whip and harness makers for the horses will lose jobs.
2. Canal boats are very important for the protection of our country.

If America goes to war with England, the canals can move the supplies very quickly.
As you may well know, railroad trains move at a great speed of 15 miles per hour. Engines are dangerous for the passengers, and they set fire to the farmlands and they scare the women, children and farm animals. God does not want people to travel at so fast a speed as 15 miles per hour.

Sincerely,
Martin VanBuren

about it. Okay. And that's basically how the majority of us react to a change that scares us. Alright, we're comfortable in a situation that you're in. Alright. He was comfortable with knowing canal boats were out there transporting people or material or whatever, and any kind of change was scary. People would lose this job and so forth. So we react a lot of times in the same way. Alright. So now that we saw some of the changes that occurred at Teamco, what kind of responses have you or others shown towards these changes? How have you responded to some of these changes? Have we been positive about all of them? When you were told that you were going to start going to classes, was everyone real excited? [2] No.

The next part of the lesson is a video of a worker who has been told that her starting time has changed, that she will need to come to work at 2:30 rather than 3 o'clock, in order to promote teamwork between shifts. The worker is not in favor of the change, especially since it means she will have to leave a training class early. The first part of the video shows her complaining to a fellow worker, and in the next part the worker talks to her manager, who explains the necessity of the change and suggests that her training class can be rescheduled. The worker accepts the manager's explanation and agrees to have her class rescheduled. The latter vignette is offered as an example of accepting change appropriately.

Following the film, Gladis tells the class that it's time for 'our role play' on how to respond to change, which she represents as an occasion 'to practise using the steps' provided in the textbook. The class is directed to divide into groups by counting off sets of three. In each group one person will pretend to be a worker who learns that additional responsibilities will be added to his job, another person acts as the worker's supervisor, and a third evaluates the worker's process. There is much confusion as the class tries to figure out what is expected in this exercise, and Gladis walks about the room giving advice and explaining the exercise again and again.

One group consisted of Aurelia, a Spanish speaker, and Hoang, who is Vietnamese (both of whom are described above), and an English- and French-speaking researcher. Aurelia didn't seem to understand the exercise, the researcher reported, but valiantly attempted to participate by focusing on the instructions in the textbook. Hoang did understand what he was supposed to do, but explained that he didn't always have the words to express his understanding. He kept laughing, blushing, and shaking his head throughout, looking from Aurelia to the re-searcher. Finally, Juan joined the group and joked to Hoang, 'Hey, tell her [Aurelia] if she doesn't do a good job she's gonna clean toilets.' Everyone laughed, and Juan continued, 'Every time I'm supervisor with this guy here I always send him to clean toilets.' Hoang then turned to Aurelia and continued the joke, 'OK, you want your new job . . . new job clean toilets.' Ironically, in the role play, Aurelia had been assigned the supervisor's role, and Hoang the worker's, but Hoang handily reversed them.

Gladis brings the class back together, asks if they have followed the steps and practised the basic principles during the role play, and then reminds everyone: 'Changes are always being made because . . . they want to improve something. Okay. Always for improvement. So, it's up to you to understand why they're happening.' The final part of the lesson consists of Gladis's directive to apply what they've learned about accepting change to their teams and to write what they've learned in their binders:

Gladis: The following is a check, the team checklist. This
is not for you, ah, to fill out right now but it's like
a reference that you can go back to once you're in
your teams. And you want to find out, especially if
there is a change, and you want it so (you) can
check yourselves to see how well you accepted it.
Go back and ask yourselves these four questions.
Did the team find out what the changes are? Did
the team find out why the changes are being
made? Did the team find out what they each have
to do? And did the team find out ways to support
the change? [If] you can answer yes to all those
questions, then you have effectively accepted the
change. If not, then you know where there's room
for improvement. Alright. And then last of all the
bottom of page five is the summary. You may
need, you may need to be very patient during some
times of change. Some members of the team will
resist change and they need your help to see how
change can benefit them—by having a positive
attitude of how I help, how can I help this work
better, you will contribute to the team's success.
You may find that the change process may be
challenging and it could be fun. And a lot of times
changes are. So, it's how we deal with them that
means the difference. If we deal with it with a
very negative (1), a lot of times you're not going
to get, uhm, a good result from it either. Alright.
So if you want good results, (always) understand it
and deal with it as best you can. Okay. Any
questions? Now we all know how to accept
change? Okay. We're going to deal with it positive,
right. Yeah. Okay. Alright. If there's no question,
let's go to the front of our books under the
Introduction section and write down one thing that
you learned today in our Pearls of Wisdom [a page
in the binder ruled off for the fifteen lessons with
spaces to record a sentence or two of what was
learned in each]. Okay. All the way to the front,
look at the little tab that says Introduction.

Female: Alright.[pages turning, 14 seconds]

Gladis: One thing that you learned in class today.
[Students writing for 2 minutes, 28 seconds]

Aurelia writes, looking back and forth from the text to the section she is supposed to fill in: 'I learn about canal boats are very important for protecting our country.' Three other workers read their more conventional 'pearls'. Gladis dismisses the class.

VI Observations on the SDWT curriculum and class

In a part of the transcript not quoted above, Gladis reminded her class of how grateful they should be to be able to take part in SDWT training. She said that other companies wouldn't invest financially in such a program, and still others wouldn't believe it could work. In many senses she is right. Fifty hours of training that draws workers off the shop floor during peak production periods to come together to learn; an elaborate system of certification and awards to continue that training; the entitlement, indeed the directive, to go forth and solve problems as a team; and the chance to present one's solutions directly to management: all these practices are laudable. We are well aware that many a company is willing to invest in training for management but continues to eschew responsibility for front-line workers, particularly when those workers are recent immigrants and when they have been relegated historically within the industry to 'non-thinking' jobs. It is important, then, to honor what was intended at Teamco and to award it its considerable due.

We are disturbed, however, by what actually emerged in practice, not just in the classes—though they are themselves a prime example—but in the implementation of the teams. One of the things about the experiment at Teamco that we most admired was its implied belief in people. The manager who was the mover and shaker behind the team concept was ready to defend the hourly workforce at every turn, expressing great faith in their abilities. He was especially proud of certain portions of the curriculum, such as the part on finance, and of his decision to expose front-line workers to the mysteries of the income statement and the balance sheet. 'This is for everyone,' he said proudly, 'the eight-dollar-an-hour, I-don't-speak-English worker. They said I was crazy.' A corporate trainer with whom we spoke likewise described the workers as Teamco's greatest asset, diligent and unfailingly loyal. And, indeed, the whole idea of a curriculum to be presented to workers during the work day in an industry governed by sudden and exacting customer demands bespeaks someone's belief in workers and in the importance assigned to their growth and development.

Unhappily, when we examine the curriculum and the pedagogy of the class described above we see another view of workers, and, we believe, a most unproductive one. This view is perhaps best summed up by the regular instructor of the class, who commented to us: 'Sometimes I feel like I am teaching children.' Indeed, the organization of the class, the participant structures in operation, the building-block approach of the curriculum—all these things are strongly reminiscent of old-style, traditionally-run classrooms for children and adolescents. They certainly don't bring to mind the education of adults who are being empowered to solve their own problems.

Let us be more specific. Even a cursory look at the complete transcript of the class shows, as do the excerpts provided above, that the vast majority of talking is done by the instructor. A closer look informed by an analysis of discourse shows that upwards of 90 percent of the conversational turns in the session (the group work being the only exception) are controlled by the instructor. This lecture format, especially considering the fact that many of the workers had difficulty with English, meant that most people never participated at all.

Training room talk can best be characterized as consisting of these mini-lectures interspersed with the most pervasive, traditional participant structure of schooling, the IRE format. In this format a teacher *initiates* a question, a student *responds* with an answer, and the teacher provides some kind of *evaluation* of the response. IRE participant structures often involve 'known answer' questions, in which the instructor knows at the outset the correct answer to the question, and is checking by means of her question whether the student can provide it. For example, in the section of the transcript in which Gladis asks the class what kind of changes the Governor of New York objected to in his letter to the US President, this exchange, typical of IRE discourse, occurs:

> *Gladis*: What were some of the changes? (INITIATION)
> *Female*: They didn't like the railroad train. (RESPONSE)
> *Male*: The train, the train. (RESPONSE)
> *Gladis*: They didn't want the railroad train. Alright.
>   (EVALUATION)

Gladis typically signalled a positive evaluation of a response with the word 'alright', varying the degree of affirmation through emphasis and tone. The effect of an IRE participant structure and 'known answer' questions, coupled with classroom activities such as calling upon people to read aloud, a classroom arrangement that has the teacher standing at the front of the room and the students seated in rows, and an approach to concepts that divides everything into what often seem like nonsensical steps—all this has the effect, we would argue, of treating the participants as infantile. Indeed, we observed some of the younger workers acting like resistant adolescents in a high school classroom, passing notes, giggling with each other, generally goofing off instead of taking the assigned tasks seriously. Add the further complication that many participants had trouble comprehending the language of instruction, English, and therefore relied on strong nonverbal cues and most likely their own memories of childhood schooling to make sense of the situation, and you have a classroom that epitomizes what Freire (1970) has called the 'banking' concept of education: students are empty receptacles with no knowledge or expertise; teachers are depositors, with an unlimited supply of knowledge and expertise, which they provide to students in a one-way 'exchange'.

The literacy practices that were part of the training drive this point home. When we first sat in on the training classes, we were amazed at the considerable literacy and language requirements of the course. There was the inhouse textbook, which made no concessions to nonnative speakers, and the language of instruction, which itself did not appear to be modified or simplified. Rather, participants were expected to read, write, and speak English at fairly sophisticated levels. Now, we have already pointed out that these expectations were unrealistic for a substantial proportion of the participants, simply because their English was still developing; Aurelia is a good example of this group. But let us assume that everyone could read, write, and speak English well enough to participate fully in the curriculum. What kinds of literacy practices were valued, and what do they suggest about the sensibilities that workers were supposed to develop as team members?

Workers were supposed to absorb the content of the textbook through their reading, and through their writing they were supposed to reproduce it. Not once in all the classes that we observed were participants ever invited to respond critically to reading material—by contrasting their own experiences with examples provided, by revealing what seemed particularly apropos and what wrongheaded, by offering additional topics to be discussed or covered. The writing activities were even more circumscribed and limiting, consisting as they did of fill-in-the-blank space types of questions, checklists, or the 'pearls of wisdom' summary of what had been learned.

It's important to remember that such activities, such approaches toward literacy and learning, send powerful implicit messages about what is expected of and what is appropriate for workers. We would argue that the message sent here is 'don't question', 'listen carefully', and 'follow directions'. It's hard to imagine a classroom structure or orientation more unlikely to suggest to participants that they are to be empowered to solve the company's problems, to be active thinkers and doers. The manager in charge of the team concept told us that the company used to 'hire people from the neck down', but that with teams 'employees will have to think; those who don't want to think will go'. The corporate trainer echoed him: 'Workers shouldn't expect always to be told what to do. You need to think for yourself what's needed and take the initiative to do it.' The SDWT training program, its curriculum, its pedagogy, and its literacy practices would seem to encourage just the opposite.

In the case of the Accepting Change class, the content of the curriculum itself promoted passivity rather than activity and initiative. Participants were directed, whenever change in their work lives occurs, to accept it appropriately by following a series of steps: find out what the changes are, why they are being made, what you have to do differently, and how to support the changes. Staggeringly, there is no urging to assess the changes or provide feedback about them. Perhaps this is a predictable stance for companies like Teamco which expect, even welcome, whatever changes are necessary to stay on top, and thus feel compelled to head off any resistance on the part of their workforce.

Ironically, though, through an SDWT session that directs workers to simply accept change, and through a hierarchy perceived as rigid despite the existence of teams, the company short-changes and short-circuits itself. As we will see in the next chapter, workers heard this lesson loud and clear, and even when changes were implemented that were clearly wrongheaded in terms of production work they 'accepted' them (which they could have done, no doubt, without a lesson on 'accepting change'). Supervisors and managers were to be obeyed when they made cleaning the toilets a priority, to borrow an example from Juan.

One more comment on the content of the Accepting Change class. There were several missed opportunities for meaningful discussion, moments when at least some of the class could have been drawn into a genuine conversation in which their opinions and ideas were valued. One of these opportunities came when Gladis asked what changes the participants had noticed during their employment at Teamco. It is clear from observations in the factory that workers are positively besieged by change on a daily basis and feel the pressure of change enormously. But these experiences were not verbalized, as Gladis, perhaps under pressure to cover the curriculum, elicited and evaluated brief, perfunctory answers.

She herself spoke at length about a change in the color, length, and laundry requirements of smocks that people wear on the job (a change that we ourselves don't see the significance of) and, when one participant attempted to explain why workers objected to not being able to wash their own smocks, Gladis rushed on. It is too bad that there was so little time for reflection in the training room, for there is certainly precious little on the shop floor. An even more important opportunity for meaningful discussion and reflection was lost during the segment that focused on the memo written by the Governor of New York, in which he objected to the loss of boat builders' and harness makers' jobs that would occur if trains took the place of canals. If there is a fear that governs the work lives of people at Teamco and other front-line employees in Silicon Valley, it is the threat of jobs disappearing through layoffs or through companies moving away.

What a productive moment this could have been, if participants had been able to compare the situation of workers during the early 1800s with their own situation today, and to go beyond the simplistic and hardhearted stance offered through the curriculum that all change is good. A potentially rich moment for critical literacy on the part of instructor and students—but it was lost. Hoang's observation about parrots seems appropriate here; just about the only response that was valued or permitted in class was a repetition of the expected.

The observations we've made about the individual session on Accepting Change hold for the other fourteen weeks of instruction that were observed. Some of the content was more conducive to self-direction and worker empowerment, such as the unit on finance and on problem-solving, but the organization of the class, the participant structures, the activities, the literacy practices, and the roles available to participants remained the same.

It is important, however, not to lay the blame for a class like Accepting Change or the others at the feet of an individual teacher. Research observations suggest that many instructors had the workers' best interests at heart; indeed, some of them attempted to circumvent or embellish the curriculum, especially in the operation of actual team meetings. However, these instructors were in the grip of a curriculum and company-imposed timelines and guidelines that gave them little leeway. In addition, the instructors were in most cases former engineers who had had no formal training as teachers, just the brief seminars offered by Teamco's training department. And this department, like those of many large corporations, looked to national vendors specializing in quality enhancement programs for most of its curriculum units, a practice that suggests that Teamco's curriculum is no anomaly in the domain of corporate training.

We should note, too, that workers experienced the curriculum in a range of ways. Juan was definitely the most enthusiastic worker the researchers came in contact with in regard to SDWT training. Others like Aurelia enjoyed the chance to practise English, even to do something a bit different from the run-of-the-mill factory day. But much more frequent were the sceptics, workers who doubted the promise of teams. As one young man put it: 'Talk [about SDWTs in classes] doesn't match reality.' Workers quickly noticed that the power differential didn't shift very much on the floor with the advent of team training. Not surprisingly, many workers seemed fairly jaded about the whole enterprise, as reflected in their jokes regarding their team-related accomplishments: 'I guess they'll make me a supervisor, now', laughed one worker whose classroom solution to an exercise was praised by the instructor.

And then there were was a small group of workers for whom the curriculum in all likelihood didn't matter a whit, for they understood very little of it due to their rudimentary English. Once, during a team meeting, a worker who was a fluent speaker of English complained about having to carry the heaviest burden for team-related duties when others on the team had graduated from SDWT training just as he had. 'Ah', said the wise team leader, 'but that does not mean that they know.'

So, what social identities were suggested through the curriculum, and what new social practices were valued? For a small minority like Juan, the team concept must have brought hope for new, more responsible roles as Teamco employees, roles that allowed greater exercise of initiative and offered different, more challenging and promising work practices. We think that Juan is unusual (an outlier), however, and that the majority of workers departed from the course the same workers they had been when they entered the training room door. They came and went as front-line employees who understood the importance of hierarchy at Teamco and their own places in it at the bottom of the heap. They understood that the training program signalled that new demands were about to be made upon them, including attending team meetings and increasing production, but they easily assimilated these new demands into their existing notions of work at Teamco. After all, quality enhancement programs were nothing new at this factory. Our assessment, then, is that SDWT training at Teamco did little to help participants create new work identities.

The Teamco training classes raise clearly the paradoxical nature of the transition to new-capitalist forms of institutional relationships. In Chapter 3 we saw school reform efforts inspired by cognitive science, efforts which have been influenced by the new work order and which resonate with many of its needs and principles. These educational movements offer 'cutting edge' pedagogies built, in part, for culturally diverse classrooms. However, at Teamco, we see a quite traditional 'transmission' pedagogy in action, certainly a pedagogy far less 'cutting edge' than the business principles that caused managers to implement it in the first place. This of course may simply represent, in part, the uneven nature of major social changes. It is also, perhaps, due to the fact that the leaders of Teamco see the classes as merely an initial and overt statement of basic principles and parameters that will be more thoroughly socialized into workers through their participation in teams as 'communities of practice' built around these principles.

The history of literacy (Graff 1987) demonstrates that literacy and, indeed, schooling in general have most often been used to inculcate in people certain values, values that represent the interests and worldviews of those who most controlled the particular forms of literacy in question. What is striking about the Teamco classes is how overt and 'bald and on record' these values are, as well as their connection to the interests of the company. One of us has argued previously (Gee 1994) that the fast-capitalist literature is quite open about the fact that worker participation and worker empowerment in the culture and values of a new-capitalist business are ultimately a *business strategy* for competitive success and, as such, constitute an overt form of hegemony in favor of the leaders and major stakeholders in the business. Of course, the paradox here, as we have seen, is that this same literature claims that new-capitalist businesses need and want workers who are 'critical' and who can 'think for themselves'.

Perhaps the root problem and the paradox are this: real education and real learning require that learners come to understand the *grounds* or *reasons* for the claims they are presented with. But learners cannot understand such grounds or reasons without engaging in real dialogue and contention about them—without knowing what it is to question them and what reasons there may be, not only for believing them, but for not believing them, as well. Such dialogue, however, is deeply problematic in the setting of a new-capitalist business where loyalty, commitment, and critical thinking, as well as allegiance to 'core values', are at bottom *economic strategies* for the business's benefit in a global hypercompetitive marketplace. In such a setting 'critical thinking' and 'commitment' can quickly become rather like *faux* antiques— having but the appearance of the real thing. Designing curricula and teaching in such a setting is bound to be a rather paradoxical affair—a paradox that the new capitalism has not as yet, in fact, solved.

After attending many weeks of SDWT classes, the researchers were all eager to get to the factory floor and observe team meetings in action. As educators, the researchers understood how difficult it is to imagine and enact a liberatory curriculum when traditional conceptions of schooling are all that most of us have experienced. Furthermore, they had a sense of the time pressures and production constraints that curriculum developers and corporate leaders were working within. The researchers had, as well, great expectations that once workers were turned out of school they would be able to accomplish a great deal more than had been apparent or expected of them in the classroom. And to a large extent this turned out to be true, as we will see shortly. However, in the same way that traditional notions of workers' roles and identities, as well as the emerging paradoxes of the new capitalism, hobbled the curriculum, they also put constraints on the operations of teams. In the next chapter we turn to actual team meetings. At the end of that chapter we reflect on why the team experiment at this factory took the shape and went the course that it did.

5   A tale of one factory: teams at work

The preceding chapter started our story of self-directed teams at an electronics assembly plant we are calling Teamco. Worker teams with a good deal of responsibility are a core feature of many new-capitalist businesses. They are intended to motivate and empower workers and thus engender full commitment to the business. They also allow for some management functions to be pushed 'down' towards the front-lines, close to where the real work is done. In addition, they allow knowledge and skills to be rendered public, distributed across people and tools, and acquired by newcomers as part of a 'community of practice'. Such teams are part of the larger aim of many new-capitalist businesses to create new worker identities and new work practices as integral aspects of a new work culture— what we called in Chapter 1 a new Discourse.

A Discourse allows people to coordinate with other people, with various tools and technologies, including literacy practices, as well as with characteristic ways of talking, acting, interacting, and valuing so as to recognize and display various social identities. Teamco sought to create a new kind of worker in a new kind of work Discourse, one recognizably part of the wider emerging Discourse of the new capital-ism (captured at a textual level in what we called, in Chapter 2, the fast capitalist literature).

However, new Discourses come into tension with old ones—tradi-tional workplace Discourses—as well as with people's other ethnic, class-based, gender-based, and community-based Discourses. Teamco (as does also the fast capitalist literature) paid little overt heed to these complex Discourse interactions, though we will certainly see them in action in a moment. Tensions between people's 'local', day-to-day, moment-by-moment goals at work and the larger 'global' goals of the business (Boden 1994), as well as between different Discourses, often embodied in one and the same people, can undo even the best intentioned social change. Whether one approves of the emerging new-capitalist work order or not, these are matters that deserve far more attention (whether to break the new order or to fix it). As we continue our case study of Teamco here, we will see them at work 'on the ground', so to speak.

Various versions of the new-capitalist Discourse are yet in transition, attempting to be born at places like Teamco. They may, indeed, not arise; something else, not yet visible, may emerge instead—something perhaps better; something perhaps worse. Day-to-day events in places like Teamco will help determine the outcome, alongside the textual work of fast capitalists and their critics.

Our description in the previous chapter of a training session at Teamco allowed us to see education 'on site' in the new capitalism with its attendant tensions and paradoxes. In this chapter we look at the teams in practice. What we see are more tensions and paradoxes. What we see, too, are complex interactions among Discourses as a new one is in the process of construction. In the end, we see both perils and promises.

I Team meetings

Teamco's training room was on the periphery of the building, off but adjacent to the shop floor. The researchers' first glimpse of the factory itself had been through a picture window near the training room, and their first impression, later confirmed, was that Teamco presented a brighter, cleaner, shinier version of other circuit board assembly plants they had visited. This industry does not operate within the stringent cleanliness requirements of, say, chip manufacturers, where workers are robed from head to foot; nonetheless, Teamco stood out as particularly tidy and orderly, testimony perhaps to its conscientious implementation of the Japanese '5S' system, and evidence certainly of the company's sense of itself as an industry icon.

The actual layout of the shop floor, on the other hand, looks a lot like that of other circuit board plants. First come the rows of expensive surface mounting machines, robots programmed to affix tiny components precisely to bare boards. These are followed by more people-intensive areas, where workers do component loading, mechanical assembly, and touch-up, all by hand. At the back of the building are testing departments, materials and kitting, and shipping. As is common in industrial plants, there are no windows bordering the floor. One of the first questions the researchers were usually asked when they arrived on the floor was about the outside: 'Is it still raining? Is it real hot today?'

The factory floor was neatly diagrammed with yellow and black tape to indicate the borders beyond which people were not allowed to walk if they weren't wearing a smock and didn't have electrostatic guards on their shoes. Interspersed among the lines of machines and work areas were computer terminals and filing cabinets which housed the all-important directions on how to assemble the boards: manufacturing process instructions or MPIs. Lining one side of the shop floor were open, movable cubicles, the natural habitat of managers, supervisors, and engineers. On the walls of the cubicles, facing the factory floor, were numerous graphs, charts, and numerical summaries describing the productivity and quality scores for every team in the building. There were also pictures of the teams that had won the building's 'team of the month' competition.

Clad in white smocks and shod with electrostatic devices, workers stood by the robots, monitoring the assembly process, or sat at tables or in front of assembly-line-like work spaces performing their handwork. Walking among them you were apt to hear rapid-fire Chinese and Vietnamese as workers conversed with each other, and heavily accented, halting English when they spoke to you. Occasionally a tall white manager would walk down the broad aisle next to the cubicles, a jarring sight indeed amid this workforce of Vietnamese, Taiwanese, Chinese, Filipinos, and other people of color.

Teams corresponded to work areas. That is, all the people who worked in shipping were on one team, all those in a handload line were on another, those in touch-up on another, and so on. Officially, each team was supposed to meet for an hour a week, every week, although this varied greatly in practice. For instance, one team from the test department met unfailingly each Monday at 7 a.m. for an hour. Other teams met sporadically or only for the researchers' benefit, and others had yet to meet at all.

Some supervisors or coaches were less than enthusiastic about the team concept, and 'hot jobs' or a heavy production schedule were apt to take precedence over meetings. When they did happen, team meetings took place in a variety of places, partly depending on the size of the team. Large teams of twenty people or so commandeered the training room, while smaller ones crowded into a cubicled conference room that abutted the factory floor, or they held their meetings at a table in the noisy cafeteria adjacent to the cubicles but off the floor.

Officially, team meetings were supposed to be conducted according to certain criteria. There was supposed to be a team leader and a minutes taker, and such people were always present in the meetings observed by the research team. These two jobs were intended to rotate among members, which sometimes happened and sometimes didn't. The team leader was not supposed to be the same person as the lead worker on the line or in an area, although this was sometimes the case, as we will see below. Ironically, there weren't supposed to be lead workers at all; these positions had been abolished with the advent of teams, when authority and responsibility on the floor were to be shared among all workers. However, in practice, leads were still leads and were recognized as such.

Each team had a binder in which minutes were recorded on pre-printed forms. There was supposed to be an agenda for each meeting, and there were recommended forms of participation, such as brain-storming and saying 'pass' if you had nothing to report. And, perhaps most importantly, team members were expected to engage in a 'seven-step problem-solving process' that had been covered in the SDWT curriculum. By means of this process, workers were supposed to analyze the causes of problems in their area (through the use of fishbone diagrams, Pareto charts and such—for details of these quality control techniques see Sashkin & Kiser 1993), to implement and evaluate a solution, and to measure the results—activities that certainly required some expertise in literacy, mathematics, and language, not to mention knowledge of manufacturing. Later, during building and plant-wide competitions, selected individual teams were expected to present the results of their problem-solving activities to management; they were judged then on their presentation style as well as their results.

One other team activity is worth previewing before we eavesdrop on an actual meeting of one team from the handload area. Shortly after we began our observation of teams, management announced plans to link self-directed work teams directly to productivity and quality results, and these results to compensation. This was done by requiring all teams to set specific quality and productivity goals for each fiscal quarter— each team completed a form containing graphs of its previous quality and productivity percentages and a rationale for its future goals. Those that met their goals were to be rewarded with a bonus.

Team leaders were expected to compute quality and productivity on a daily basis, to record these scores daily in a computer program with a security system (to prevent cheating), and to report back to the team, so that problems affecting their scores might be solved. Then, at the end of the quarter, the money available for bonuses would be divided equally among teams that had met their goals; those that had not met their goals would receive nothing.

There was naturally some interest, and worry, on the part of workers about this new system. In the past, bonuses of varying amounts had simply appeared in the pay envelope of some individuals. Under the old system the rationale for determining bonuses was never made explicit, though everyone had a theory—it's how much overtime you're willing to put in or it's how well you get along with your supervisor. With the advent of teams, individual performance would cease to be rewarded in favor of the team unit; no matter how hard individuals might work, their fortunes would rise or fall with those of their team. It follows, then, that one important potential activity for team meetings would be setting goals and monitoring weekly performance on quality and productivity, with an eye toward determining whether or not team performance was likely to result in a team bonus.

It would be impossible to choose a typical team or a typical team meeting to present here, for there was great variety at Teamco. Some teams seemed to model themselves on SDWT training or management meetings, with a person at the front of the room directing the meeting in a formal way, while others were much more casual, eschewing an agenda or rules for participation. Sometimes supervisors (now called coaches) took an active part in the meetings of the teams in their areas, and sometimes they didn't.

Teams varied as well according to ethnicity, gender, and the education and work experience of participants, mainly because teams were organized by department or work area. Some departments (such as testing) required more education of their workers than did others; some were known to be places primarily for female workers (like handload); still others were segregated by ethnicity (recall that the touch-up area where Aurelia and Hoang worked was predominately Vietnamese). Some of these distinctions were driven by the values and beliefs of workers, who constructed and enforced culturally based notions of what constitutes an appropriate job in terms of gender and ethnicity.

The team we will listen to shortly came from handload, an entry-level section of the plant. The work doesn't require much training, although all workers in this area must take 'basic electronics' at Teamco Tech once they become permanent employees. Workers in this area place components on boards by hand. The process begins when a line is assigned a batch of boards from a customer (such as Intel or Hewlett-Packard or 3Com). The lead worker decides how to partition the work among the six people in her line; for example, how many and what kind of components the first person in the line will load. The boards are pushed from one end of the line to the other, with each worker adding a new set of components.

In front of each worker is a color-coded diagram, indicating schematically which parts should go where. The last person on the line is the QC, or quality control; she inspects the work done by the others and when necessary refers to a set of manufacturing process instructions, the major document on the floor, as does the lead worker. Written by engineers, these instructions describe what workers are supposed to do in each factory department or area in order to assemble a given circuit board. After inspection the QC loads the boards onto a cart, and they are wheeled off to the next department.

While the others are assembling and inspecting the parts the lead worker continues to organize the work, troubleshoot, or help out on the line. The pace is intense. There are time standards for each board and contradictory pressures on the workers, both to work faster and to work cleaner, increasing productivity and reducing the number of defects—all part and parcel of meeting team goals.

Our handload team, which called itself 'Acon' after a major customer, consisted of seven women, several of whom are introduced below. The first two, Xuan and Eva, played a big role in the team meeting that we are to discuss.

> *Xuan* was of Chinese heritage. She grew up in Vietnam and spoke
> Vietnamese as well as Cantonese fluently, but lacked confidence in her
> English, which she had begun to acquire when she arrived in the
> United States four years earlier. Young, in her twenties, she was small
> and soft-spoken, and although she was the lead of her handload line
> and in charge of her team's meetings as well, she often had trouble
> influencing the workers to participate in team activities. The supervisor
> of the handload lines reported that Xuan had no desire to be promoted,
> but we noted that Xuan had ungrudgingly taken on more and more
> responsibilities regarding teams and their reporting requirements and
> that she had become quite adept at handling the growing paperwork
> surrounding goal-setting. She had also used every opportunity to learn
> English, although shyly. Her team had the best quality and productivity
> scores of the handload area, with almost perfect quality scores, or zero
> defects, and productivity that sometimes ranged over 100 percent. Xuan
> was engaged to be married; she and her fiance were planning a

traditional Chinese wedding celebration at a local restaurant in the coming year.

Eva, the most recent hire in Xuan's handload line, was originally from the Philippines. Her English was very, very good, and because of this she was the informal spokesperson for the team, despite the fact that Xuan was its leader and Eva the most recent hire. Eva was also responsible on most occasions for taking minutes during the meetings. Married with two children, she often commented that she had two jobs, one at Teamco and one when she went home to be a wife and mother. Eva was hired as a temporary, as are all workers at Teamco, and during the time of the research she was very proactive in attempting to be made permanent. When all the other members of her line refused to take on the tedious, eye-straining job of quality inspector, she eventually volunteered for it, for the supervisor had hinted broadly that it would help her chances. Although she claimed to be afraid to talk to the supervisor and often asked the researchers to intervene on her behalf, Eva was quite outspoken at team meetings and on the line—so much so, in fact, that she regularly offended some of her co-workers. Eva was made permanent about five months after she was first hired, much earlier than is the norm.

Sau Ling was from Burma and missed her homeland very much, having left most of her family there a few years earlier. She was the person most offended by Eva's loud comments about defects on the boards. Her most extended conversations with the researchers concerned her anger and hurt at being blamed for quality problems that she hadn't caused. Extremely quiet during team meetings, she rarely participated but appeared to listen intently and to understand everything.

Mrs Chen, the oldest member of the team, was also its 'pariah', sitting off to one side during meetings and rarely interacting with her co-workers on the line. She was rumored to be rich and to work at the factory as a 'hobby', and she was much maligned by the other workers for her failure to cooperate and for being too slow at her work. Mrs Chen sometimes punctuated team meetings with loud bursts of complaints, spoken in such heavily accented and rapid English that it sounded Chinese. During these moments the team members would either ignore her, laugh, or roll their eyes.

Irene, a Filipina, was the mother of two grown daughters and a five-year-old son, pictures of whom she kept in a plastic cube at her work station (a practice officially prohibited for the sake of safety and neatness). Her husband was American-born; she had met him in the Philippines. Irene didn't take part in the meetings and often refused team-related requests, such as taking minutes or thinking about goals at home. She seemed, in fact, uninterested in work and resentful of efforts to engage her more fully in team-related activities. However, she understood the monetary implications of goal-setting quite well, and she also calculated her overtime pay precisely, comparing her earnings with those of her co-workers. She and Eva sat next to each other on the line and on occasion spoke Tagalog to each other.

Lan was the young supervisor/coach of the Acon team and three other handload lines. In her late twenties, small and attractive, she was a dynamo on the floor, rushing about, directing the work in rapid Vietnamese or determined English, furiously filling out paperwork, afraid of no one but feared by many. Lan had immigrated to the United States from Vietnam in 1989, and she lived in San José with her parents and three siblings. She got a job at Teamco shortly after arriving, started out in handload, and then was promoted to lead. About one year before our visits she was promoted to supervisor; she told us at that time she didn't know much about what to do but had since learned a lot on her own. Lan was attending classes at a local community college in ESL, computers, and fashion design; she hoped eventually to be an engineer. She would like to get married some day, but rejected many of the traditional Chinese values of her parents, particularly their notions of saving money. Later she changed her name, dropping 'Lan' and taking 'Angela' instead.

The meeting we are to examine took place after the Acon team had been meeting regularly for four months. Most, but not all, of the team members had completed SDWT training; one notable exception was Eva, who was a recent hire and still classified as a temporary employee ineligible for the training. The meeting was held in the cafeteria at 2 p.m., one hour before day shift ended, and while other workers from various departments were milling about the room. All the participants described above, plus a few others, were present, with the exception of Lan, the supervisor, who preferred to let the teams run on their own. The researcher had attended almost every meeting of the Acon team thus far, had come to know everyone, and was viewed by most as a friendly resource.

As we did in the last chapter, with the transcript of the classroom lesson, we present here a summary of the team meeting punctuated with excerpts of actual talk, the intention being to give a vivid account of what the meeting was like. The questions to keep in mind during this section include: What does this meeting suggest about the identities that workers are constructing as team members? That is, what patterns of talking, acting, and valuing are apparent, what social practices? And how might we describe the literate demands of such meetings and workers' responses to them? That is, how are these demands embedded within the company's experiment with teams, and how do workers meet those demands, circumvent them, or shape them?

This meeting of the Acon team began, as they all did, with the team's exodus from the shop floor to the cafeteria. Team leader Xuan went round from station to station quietly, but insistently, announcing in a high-pitched voice: 'Team meeting, team meeting!' The researchers walked with Eva, as was their custom, for she enjoyed providing quick summaries of what had been happening the previous week. Eva confided that she had given Lan an 'ultimatum' about being made permanent. When asked what she had told her exactly, Eva confessed that she had written her a note, being afraid to speak to her face to face, and that she had explained she would have to leave Teamco if she were not made permanent soon.

The group gathered around a cafeteria table in the usual manner, with Xuan and Eva at one end next to the researchers, the others grouped near us, and Mrs Chen some distance away. The first part of the meeting was a recital of the week's problems, common fare for any handload line. There was the big board which required each person on the line to load 59 components apiece, and the additional problem of having had twenty of these boards returned to the line because certain parts had been reversed. There was the problem on another board of 'mixed parts', the mistaken use of one part of the same size and color as another but of a different value; and the problem of 'bent legs', the disturbance of the tiny wires protruding from components that fit down into the board.

Here is an excerpt:

> *Eva*: [to researcher] Oh, we're having a hard time doing the Lexicon, the big board. The one Lan told you had more than 300 components.
>
> *Xuan*: 375.
>
> *Eva*: One person, you have to load 59 components at every station.
>
> *Researcher*: One person?
>
> *Eva*: We spent two hours finding our own location.[Much laughter]

> *Xuan*: Yeah, ( ) the location, one minute, the other side [miming with her hands finding the locations on the board]
> *Eva*: We did about 20 boards from 8 to 3, and then the next, the following day they returned to us, reverse [meaning the line had made a mistake, putting the parts on in the wrong direction].[Laughter]

All this talk proceeded casually, with much laughter and joking and with no one taking control of the meeting or enforcing an order of business, though Eva with her good English and strong personality tended to dominate. Interspersed among the discussions of typical handload problems were other topics of interest—a startled realization that someone had forgotten to bring the book for taking minutes, a critical observation about the short dress of a cleaning person who walked past the table, a report of a rumor that more lines were soon to be added, a complaint about a noxious smell in the wave area.

After Eva mentioned John, a Filipino worker who said he didn't want to work in the wave area because of the smell, there was a pause of several seconds until Xuan brought up the issue of productivity. One day the previous week, it seems, their line had had a productivity score of only 55 percent, which was below their stated goal for the quarter. Xuan explained that 'the lady', by whom she meant the female engineer, thought the calculation might be wrong, that it should be higher, and Eva urged Xuan to make the correction. Xuan stated, however, that it was too late, implying that once recorded the score couldn't be changed. Here is their exchange (which includes overlapping and interrupted conversational turns, indicated respectively by a dash and by spacing):

> *Eva*: Did you check the lady about the fifty-five percent-
> *Researcher*: Mhm.
> *Eva*: of what we did, ah, just any [ ]-
> *Mai*: Just any [ ]?
> *Eva*: And he told you to check it to the lady. So did you check it?
> *Xuan*: Yeah, I check already.
> *Eva*: What did she said?
> *Xuan*: She said it might wrong, you know, because [ ]-
> *Eva*: That's what, so how many percent now?
> *Xuan*: [slight pause] You cannot change it.
> *Eva*: Aaaaaahhh.

After this exchange, Xuan continued to focus the group's attention on poor productivity, pointing out that on one day in the current week the line's score was only 57 percent. Eva's agitated question 'Why, why, why?' brought a quick and spirited explanation, constructed jointly—in fact almost simultaneously—by several people on the team. The complete transcript of this exchange follows, but its gist is this. The Acon line had been asked to load components on a new board, the Acuson, during a period of enforced idleness (the melting machine was down, making their customary boards unavailable). The Acuson was a board ordinarily loaded by another line, and the Acon team wasn't familiar with it. The board was especially complex, requiring 21 pieces of transistor and much tedious masking. There were only five people on the Acon line to do this work, whereas the line that usually loaded this board had seven workers. Nonetheless, the Acon line managed to complete 120 Acuson boards, working two hours of overtime. But their productivity was below their goal.

We present the following long and rather complex excerpt because it gives a sense of how talk typically happened in the meeting, although the conversational turns occurred much more quickly than can be suggested on the page—one right after another, after another. We make no attempt to display the complex overlappings of talk; as above we simply use a hyphen (-) to show cases where talk latched on to or overlapped with other talk. The excerpt also indicates how savvy the workers were as a group, even those like Dau whose spoken English was quite limited and who didn't ordinarily participate in meetings. They knew precisely why their productivity was low for that day, and could marshal all sorts of details and evidence in support of their explanation, albeit in a somewhat rowdy, random manner.

> *Xuan*: -But this week, this week had one day is
> fifty-seven, right?
> *Woman*: Yeah-
> *Dau*: -Ah why? Ah why? Why?
> *Xuan*: Because [slight pause], us don't have job, right?
> *Dau*: Yeah-
> *Eva*: -I can show more.
> *Dau* (and *Xuan*): I can show more-
> *Eva*: -Ohhhh, yeah.
> *Dau*: One hundred twenty.
> *Eva*: Ah huh, we did ah-
> *Dau*: -wh-

Eva: -Acuson board I think-

Dau: -What hour, what hour-

Eva: -Wednesday.

Researcher: Ah, when could you did twenty boards-

Women: -[laughter]-

Researcher: -that day? [laughter trails into next sentence] Is that the day you're talking about? The day you did twenty?-

Dau: -First number wa-was-

Eva: No that's different this week.

Researcher: Oh, this week oh, oh, oh. That was last week-

Xuan: -I think we

Eva: -We don't have boards because the melting machine was down-

(Dau): -[voice in background]-

Eva: -and they let us do the Acuson board and they spent I don't know how many hours we did their board.

Researcher: Is it, you don't usually do Acuson-

Xuan: -(Over) two hour you're not, overtime two hour, they have (eighty) [ ] but us, how many, how-

Dau: -One hundred twenty.

Xuan: One hundred twenty.

Dau: How how how how how long. I don't know how long-

Xuan: -I remember-

Dau: -may maybe-

Xuan: -five hour-

Eva: -five hour-

Dau: -maybe five, maybe five, maybe-

Eva: -maybe four to five hour-

Dau: -maybe so[Voices mix and laughter]-

Researcher: -Why that?

Eva: Because (there were) so many defect board.

Woman: -[in Vietnamese]

Researcher: -You're not used to doing that?

Eva: No, it's because this (is) Acuson board-

Researcher: -Oh, so you don't do that Acuson board-

Eva: -Especially we're just trying to help because we don't have any board to do.

Researcher: So it took you a long time. That made your productivity low.

Xuan: (softly) Yeah.

Researcher: Would, mhm-

Mai: -Yeah-

Researcher: -So-
      Xuan: -Just how how many person?
     (Eva): Ten.
      Dau: -One, two, three, four, five, five, five, five people.
     Xuan: -Acuson. [pause] Five people.
      Dau: Five people.
    (Xuan): Nah, [Vietnamese spoken]
      Dau: -five people Acuson.[Vietnamese spoken throughout
         above]
Researcher: Oh, Acuson usually has seven-
      Dau: -Yeah.
Researcher: And you, and just five of you guys-
      Dau: -Yeah-
    (Xuan): -And-
      Mai: -Twenty, twenty, twenty, twenty-one-
      Eva: -transistor, take the pieces of transistor you have-
  Woman: Ouh-
      Eva: -to put masking on it-
Researcher: Oh-
      Eva: -Just-
     Xuan: But it's hard to know. You need to pick the (state).
         If you (fall out like that) you cannot.

The next topic in the meeting was how to document this problem. Eva stated loudly to Xuan, 'You have to put a note on the paper . . . you have to give them a reason', meaning that Xuan should take care to write down on their score sheet an explanation for the low productivity score for that particular day. Xuan defended herself, saying she usually wrote these things down but on that day she simply forgot. Eva retorted with spirit that Xuan might have forgotten to write but she would remember the bonus—and maybe the team wouldn't get one:

      Eva: Then you have to make a note at the back and tell
         them the reason why is our productivity so low
         that day. So they will give us credit for that-
    Xuan: -I know, yeah, this time I forgot.
     Eva: Ay-yai-yai![Much laughter all around]
     Eva: Did you see every time, did you see every time we
        have a meeting or something else I put a note on
        my paper?
    Xuan: Yeah-
     Eva: -Yeah you have to do that all the time.[17 related
        turns omitted]
    Xuan: I write a note already.
Researcher: Good.

> *Xuan*: But that Acuson I forget [laugh].
> *Researcher*: [laugh] You forgot the Acuson.[Much laughter]
> *Researcher*: Okay [pause].
>   *Eva*: You'll remember the bonus.[Much laughter]
>   *Eva*: [teasingly] Maybe we don't receive any.[Much laughter]

The meeting began to wind down. Eva asked jokingly whether anyone had been fighting—'Everybody fighting?'—a reference to the rather steady history of conflicts between Mrs Chen and the rest. Mrs Chen responded, 'Everybody tired', which prompted a whispered conversation about Mrs Chen's rumored wealth and some raucous comments on what she could do about her high blood pressure.

Eva then turned the conversation one last time back to their productivity for the week, asking Xuan: 'How many percent we have this week?' Although she didn't have the numbers at hand, Xuan, with help from the team, was able to reconstruct from memory their scores for the first three days of the week: 77 percent on Monday, the infamous 57 percent on Tuesday, and 75 percent on Wednesday. The data hadn't been analyzed for Thursday, but the group felt confident that their score was fine for that day.

The researcher averaged these data and reported that their score was 69 percent thus far for the week, well above their quarterly goal of 60 percent. Xuan then consulted a little black notebook that she always carried in her pocket and announced that for the entire quarter thus far their productivity average was 82 percent, but their quality was poor, that it was still a problem. No one commented. The half hour set aside for the meeting had passed and the Acon team wandered back to the floor, chatting in groups of two or three as they walked.

II Teamwork revisited

This meeting of the Acon team certainly does not fit usual notions of a formal meeting, at least the notions of those accustomed to some variation on Robert's Rules of Order. Nor does it abide by the guidelines set up by Teamco through its SDWT curriculum. There's no agenda, no apparent order of events. There's no problem-solving *à la* fishbone diagrams and Pareto charts or any other reminder of the SDWT classes. There's no one really in charge. People wander in and out of the conversation, paying attention to what interests them, ignoring the rest. Talk is simultaneous, overlapping, and latched, as one person repeats the words of the current speaker or finishes someone else's sentence or interrupts or talks on top of another. There is much laughter and joking.

One of the graduate-student researchers, who had lived in Southeast Asia and spoke fluent Vietnamese, told us that the meeting transported him to Vietnam, that the participants were very 'close' to that culture, not yet being completely Americanized, and that they seemed to draw on common Vietnamese participant structures. It seemed to us, as well, that there was something reminiscent here of kitchen-table conversations among women everywhere, something most of us have witnessed or experienced.

Although the meeting may appear to have been chaotic, with some of the members less than cooperative and others sublimely unaware of Teamco's Basic Principles, it is noteworthy that some important work of the team was getting done. One can point, for example, to a litany of handload problems at the beginning of the meeting, dutifully noted in the minutes—reversed parts on board number 158294, bent legs on number 4929194—a significant step in identifying the line's quality problems.

Then there is the jointly constructed explanation for their low productivity on one particular day—they were working on a complex board foreign to them, and their line was short of the requisite number of workers. This explanation allowed them to account for a problem if not to fix it. And there is the Acon team's discussion of how to document these extenuating circumstances, so as not to be penalized on their productivity record and, ultimately, their team-based bonus and team-worthy activities.

The fact that so much was accomplished in this informal, folksy gathering, and that there was participation by workers who did not speak in other forums that the researchers had observed, makes one wary of imposed notions of what counts as a good meeting. Indeed, we witnessed less lively, more dreary gatherings of other teams that did abide by the letter of the law as to how to conduct a meeting, but accomplished less.

Another indication that the Acon workers were acquiring the sensibilities to operate as a team is their attention to documentation. The enormous reporting apparatus associated with productivity and quality scores for teams, alluded to in the above transcript, especially in Eva's comments, underlines the increasing role of literacy in this factory and the ways in which writing, reading, and computation took their place in day-to-day work events.

Every week, it seemed, engineers or supervisors would invent a new form or revise an old one, most of them designed to enforce careful recording and analysis of data collected on productivity and quality rates. The data were then transferred to computer programs, which generated the myriad graphs and charts that lined the cubicle walls. For the most part, lead workers buckled down and mastered the massive new reporting requirements, attending the meetings in which new forms and methods of calculation were introduced, computing their scores and filling out their forms each day after work with a bottle of 'white-out' nearby, and acquiring the technological sophistication needed to wade through and modify vast computerized data bases.

They also groaned—'No, not another form! So much paper!'—and noted that the paperwork was an additional burden in an already burdened work day. Workers were also quick to notice the ways in which they could turn paperwork to their advantage. Eva's zeal in writing down explanations for the team's low productivity is a good example. Xuan's little black book of important numbers and facts is another. And when faced with strict reporting requirements that rigidly divided the day and the work into unworkable segments, workers learned to fudge, altering what they reported so that it would fit the forms.

One could say, then, that a part of the new working identities of people on the front-line at Teamco had much to do with literacy and numeracy. Suddenly, not only were handloaders expected to be quick and accurate at their work, they were also, with the advent of teams and new systems of reporting and monitoring, supposed to conceptualize their work differently. They were now to include as part of it an understanding of goals, goal-setting, calculations, and reports, with all the literate acts these activities entail.

Put another way, workers were asked to conceive of themselves, not just as employees who performed the physical act of placing components on a board but also as thinkers, as people who monitored their own handloading rates, reflected on and analyzed their problems, and reported the same through print and through presentations. A literacy lover's delight. The clever new knowledge worker. The enchanted workplace?

People who make their living with language are apt to be pleased with the wider literacy requirements of Teamco, viewing the practices as potentially humanizing or even liberating. At the very least, they are likely to point out, this kind of work is better than the familiar 'hire them from the neck down' policy that characterized workplaces of old.

We would also point out that the competent ways in which workers tackled the mounting paperwork, adapted to the new reporting requirements, and even modified or adjusted or appropriated those requirements in small ways, speaks volumes about workers' abilities. The faith of the manager in charge of teams was well placed; these workers rose to the challenge.

But let us press a little further, situating the literacy practices that evolved at Teamco within the larger context of work at the factory. When we analyzed transcripts of the Acon meeting and those of other teams, our purpose was twofold. First, we wanted to understand how literacy was used: who was expected to read and write, in what situations, and for what purposes? Second, we wanted to understand how teams functioned: what was the range of their activities; in what ways were the meetings a forum for solving problems and taking action, and in what ways were team members constrained?

One of the analysis codes that we assigned *infrequently*, both in the Acon meetings and in meetings of other teams, was 'Taking Responsibility', which we defined as 'making a decision and acting upon it either individually or as a group'. We thought that this category might capture something fundamental to the notion of self-directed work teams. But the only example of such an action in the Acon meeting was Eva's description of the letter she wrote to her supervisor asking to be made permanent, and this was an individual action not a team-based or team-related effort.

A more frequently used code in Acon and other meetings was 'Explaining' (i.e. describing a work situation or work process in such a way as to identify problems) and 'Complaining' (i.e. commenting upon a work situation or work process in such a way as to emphasize how it is problematic or in order to assign blame). The list of handload quality problems generated at the beginning of the Acon meeting fits the 'complaining' category; the discussion of low productivity we coded as 'explaining'.

This type of analysis was helpful in that it required us to be more precise in identifying the kinds of activities that actually occurred in team meetings and the kinds that were absent. In general, we found that meetings, at their best, included some identification and analysis of problems encountered on the floor. Sometimes this happened formally, with fishbone diagrams and such, and sometimes it happened informally, as in the Acon meeting.

However—and this is the rub—action was rarely if ever taken by the teams regarding the problems they uncovered. In the worst and most common scenario, problems were identified and characterized but were never mentioned again. Thus the Acon team might complain about defective parts, they might explain the production practices that resulted in their reduced productivity, but they never did anything about the problems themselves. Documenting the reasons for their low productivity rate was as close as they came to taking action. More rarely, lead workers would promise to 'look into' an issue, usually by consulting with a supervisor or an engineer, leaving the other workers out of the loop and maintaining the traditional hierarchy.

Now, there are several possible explanations for this gap we witnessed so often—between workers conceptualizing a problem and being able to take action on it. One can argue that teams simply didn't know how to take the next step, that they hadn't learned this crucial skill in the SDWT curriculum. One might conjecture that team members had no time to engage in problem-solving missions, so bound were they to production goals. One might find fault with the kinds of problems that workers identified, which tended to focus outside their own areas rather than within them.

We think the most robust explanation, however, has to do with the culture of the company itself and its apparent desire to 'empower' workers while continuing to tightly control them, a tension we identified in the last chapter. The identities that workers constructed, and the identities that the company appeared to value for its workers, despite its investment in 'self-directed' work teams, foregrounded a willingness to follow instructions and accept change without question, rather than to ask questions and problem-solve.

Once, in a meeting of another team, we witnessed a discussion among the team members, the team lead, and Lan, the supervisor, regarding a new manufacturing rule recently imposed by management. The gist of this rule was that, whatever the job that workers were carrying out, it should be done by at least two people on the line. The thinking was that two sets of hands are better than one, that two will get the work done faster than one. This rule may have worked well in many situations, but it led to ridiculous and counterproductive work practices in others.

For example, sometimes this particular team, which specialized in mechanical insertion of larger parts into boards, had small jobs to deal with; that is, the manufacturing process instructions would call for their area to attach only one or two parts or to put masking on one or two sections. In these situations it was more time-consuming to divide the work among two people than for one person to take total charge of it.

But under the new rule one person must put on a strip of tape, then hand the board to another person, who puts on another strip.

During the team's discussion of this new work rule there was much laughter and joking about its silliness and more than a few complaints and worries. 'They keep on changing the rules every day', noted one worker. 'I don't want to contradict my manager', said the lead. However, there was no suggestion, no discussion whatsoever that management be apprised of the difficulty and advised to change the rule. This was not part of the culture of the factory, despite its organization into 'self-directed' work teams.

A few days after the team meeting the researcher had a chance to ask the lead worker about the rule and why workers weren't authorized to determine when and when not to apply it. Mr Marcos, a retired dentist from the Philippines and a father figure to his younger team members, merely shrugged and said with some resignation: 'Management decides.' Workers should be able to decide how to arrange the equipment and the tools, he believed, because they know the most about them, but management decides. While it is a basic tenet of the fast-capitalist literature that new-capitalist businesses must exploit—build upon—workers' knowledge (especially the 'tacit knowledge' gained in practice), our case study shows how difficult this can be in real institutional settings. It requires radically new institutions, new leaders, and new workers.

Literacy practices were also implicated in this culture where management decides. We cited some instances above of workers taking charge of literacy, so to speak, not only acquiring the various practices valued at the company but turning writing to their own purposes—creating a paper trail (to use the example above) documenting a reasonable explanation for their low productivity on a given day. We must point out, however, that for the most part the kind of literacy valued in the factory emphasized self-monitoring, not self-direction, and that workers had no choice but to abide by rigid documentary rules—recall Xuan being resigned to the fact that, once entered into the computer, her team's productivity score couldn't be changed even if it were wrong. Leads spent inordinate amounts of time counting and figuring and tabulating, all in service of accountability.

On the one hand, self-directed work teams were supposed to be empowered to solve their own problems. However, on the other hand, managers and engineers appeared so compelled to measure and document quality and productivity, to find ways to quantify the teams' work, to keep tabs and to keep track—all through literacy-related activities, we might add—that workers were left very little room in which to maneuver.

One more literacy-related example will make this point. We mentioned earlier that manufacturing process instructions (MPIs) were the central documents on the shop floor. Written by engineers, there was a set of these instructions for each individual circuit board. They outlined the manufacturing process from beginning to end, for each department or area, and listed the type, amount, and serial number of each component to be affixed to the board. These central documents were consulted when engineers determined standard times, or how long it should take to complete a given piece of work on a board. And these standard times, of course, influenced productivity scores.

It was well known on the factory floor that MPIs were often wrong or outdated. Busy engineers just didn't always have the time to make corrections, or they overlooked tiny details that nonetheless made the difference between a board that worked and one that failed or between your achieving the productivity goal for the day and missing it. Despite the fact that they knew about the problems with the MPIs, workers were absolutely prohibited from changing them, from making an alteration even of the smallest kind.

On one afternoon the researchers were watching Xuan as she studied one MPI. She eventually found the problem that she was looking for: the author had mistakenly written a '1' where an '11' should have been in the column listing the number of components. This simple mistake had major implications for Xuan's line in terms of productivity calculations. It obviously takes eleven times longer to load eleven components than it takes to load one; the group's 'standard time', or the amount of time allotted for assembling that board, was thus way off kilter, and so would be their productivity if they went ahead and assembled the board as it had to be done if it were to function.

One of the researchers reached over with a pencil and attempted to write in the other numeral, whereupon the usually docile Xuan gave a startled shriek and ordered us away, explaining that we must not, the workers must not, even Lan the supervisor must not, modify an MPI. She and her group went ahead and assembled the boards so that they would work, and suffered the consequences. Other workers took a different approach, refusing to make changes they knew were needed when an MPI was incorrect, even if the engineer gave verbal permission to do so. 'Don't go by verbal, go by written', Mr Marcos warned his group again and again, having been burnt once too often.

In some ways, then, the literacy practices of the factory—who was enabled to read and write what documents for what purposes on what occasions—were a window on the work practices of the factory as a whole and the hierarchical structures that governed them. Despite the fact that Teamco required its workforce to organize around teams, required those teams to meet, and required them to problem-solve and to continually find ways to improve and document their quality and productivity, despite the fact that it claimed to want a thinking work-force, a self-directed, and empowered one, the researchers saw contin-ual evidence that workers received a conflicting message. They were, in fact, quite constrained in terms of the actions they could take, the decisions they could make, the influence they could have, and the literacies they could practice.

III Conclusion and coda: a team competition

Early on in our research the upper level manager who had been responsible for introducing and pushing the notion of teams at Teamco remarked to us that this experiment, this cultural change, would suc-ceed, and for three reasons. First, he told us, 'People are realistic', they know their jobs are going away and consequently they must interest themselves in their company's efforts to remain competitive and suc-cessful. Second, he said, 'people want to be part of something excel-lent'—at this point he cited the NUMI anecdote with which we began the previous chapter, the story of the auto worker who left a note on the windshield of a car that he proudly recognized as his own making. And last, the manager told us, the reorganization around teams would succeed because 'people respond to trust and respect'.

This analysis of why the team concept would ultimately succeed at Teamco is remarkable for the tensions and contradictions it reveals. On the one hand, there is a tough economic realism, to wit the manager's depiction of a brutish marketplace where the choice for workers is between 'bad and worse' rather than 'good and bad', as he put it on this same occasion. Jobs are leaving the United States by the hundreds of thousands, and the implication is that if workers at Teamco want to keep theirs they'll cooperate. On the other hand, juxtaposed with this tough and no doubt accurate scenario, is the manager's humanistic belief in and appeal to people's abilities, motivations, and aspirations, their desire to be part of something excellent. On another occasion he told us that he had no doubt that 95 percent of the workers at Teamco had the ability to carry out the team experiment successfully.

So, at Teamco, workers and managers alike must be Janus-faced. Managers, on the one side, must do whatever is necessary to keep their company afloat; on the other, they must treat their employees with trust and respect, for this is the way for a business to succeed these days. For their part workers, on the one side, must recognize that they work for a company driven by market forces and having the profit motive to be as ruthless as necessary towards its own employees; on the other side, they must realize that their bosses are now treating them with trust and respect, and respond appropriately with an even greater commitment to the company.

This is the double-edged message of the new capitalism, at least in its transitional state—the contradiction within talk about non-authoritarian work structures, distributed knowledge systems, and the democratization of work. One has to wonder how deeply the proposed changes will penetrate, how seriously or successfully they can be enacted, given that there is at the heart of all new-capitalist reorganizations of work, as at Teamco, a hard and inescapable tension. This is that the humanistic, democratic reforms are being enacted, not because they create more humanistic, less hierarchical conditions for workers but because they are viewed as the way to create more and/or continuing profit.

Given this contradiction, one would expect trouble in paradise. One would expect, for example, that workers would be treated with respect and trust only in the most superficial of ways, and that old patterns of relating and being would be superimposed on new practices, distorting their purpose and changing their values. The way in which any company creates and sustains a particular vision of a work culture will of course be complicated and shaped by a range of local factors—the composition of the workforce, their cultures, genders, and personal, educational, and work histories, as well as the company's history and its accustomed ways of relating to its employees. But we would argue that a major part of what was happening in the classes and the curriculum for self-directed work teams at Teamco, as well as during team meetings and work on the shop floor, had also to do with contradictions that lie at the heart of the new capitalism.

We leave you with one last image of Teamco, one that captures many of the tensions and contradictions we have discussed in this chapter. This image could easily turn into another apocryphal tale told in the media and spread among corporate trainers and CEOs, were it not situated in research of the sort we have illustrated here. The last step in the team process at this factory was a presentation to management, both at quarterly competitions held in each division of the factory and at monthly management meetings held at the company headquarters. If the quarterly competitions were equivalent to 'opening in Peoria', the researchers were told, the monthly presentations were the corporate equivalent of bigtime Broadway.

The researchers watched these presentations and were greatly impressed. They saw white-smocked workers stand in front of a room full of suits, their charts and graphs carefully prepared and in hand, their speeches rehearsed and memorized. Most were clearly nervous and ill at ease as they went through their prescribed paces—identifying their teams, explaining their seven-step problem-solving process, displaying their data on quality and productivity, and fielding questions at the end—many of them coping valiantly with less than perfect English.

There was something wonderful about these meetings, these spaces where workers and managers came in touch, where front-line employees did the talking and explaining, where managers could ask but not direct. Perhaps as academics fond of and accustomed to such public displays of literate abilities, we romanticize these presentations a little too much. But still, the image was powerful and, we expect, would affect others similarly. It represented the coming together of groups in the corporate world who are normally divided from each other by vast social, economic, and cultural gulfs, and it reversed the power differential for at least a moment by at least a little. And it should lay the foundation for the formation of new work identities and new social practices.

What the researchers found, however, when they looked more closely at these team competitions, was that old work identities and old social practices were nonetheless very much in place. Many teams were never asked or allowed to participate in these presentations, due to a complex system of requirements and eliminations. It turned out that the teams that could benefit the most from the discipline of preparation, such as Xuan's handload line, were the ones least likely to be chosen. Of those teams selected to present and compete, most team members had nothing to do with the process. Supervisors and team leaders tended to construct and choreograph the presentations, supplying the data and the charts and the script. While the presenters benefited at least from the experience of preparing and speaking to management, most workers remained aloof from the process. The whole affair began to take on the flavor of a dog and pony show.

But perhaps the deepest problem with the presentations was the added layer of competitions. In the quarterly divisional meetings, and in the company-wide year-end finale, teams competed against each other, were graded by a committee of managers, and were awarded monetary prizes. While the winners were happy on such occasions, the losers were very bitter indeed, and often questioned the legitimacy of the scoring process. This wasn't just sour grapes on their part.

In one such competition, in which one team would be selected to represent the division at an upcoming company-wide competition, three teams lined up against each other. Of the three, one had worked long and hard to come up with new material, new problems solved, and so on while the other two used the same presentation they had won with in the past. It turned out that the team that presented new material, and that in truth embodied the best of what teams are supposed to be about, came in last, in part because their presentation style was less polished.

A conversation that the researchers had with Carlos, the team leader of the last-place team, revealed the effect that such inequities have on workers' morale, and also reminds us one more time of what the team experience is like from a front-line worker's point of view. When the researchers visited the factory the week after the competition, Carlos had cancelled his group's team meeting (after which one member clapped and almost ran back to her station to tell the others).

He pointed out that the group had been meeting regularly for almost nine months, that they were tired and needed a break. He also noted that other teams never met, yet they received their quarterly bonuses, which made his own group question whether meetings were really necessary. Carlos went on to express his dismay at the results of the competition, given that the other presenters had merely relied on old material.

The conversation became more and more wide-ranging, as Carlos expressed his concern that managers and supervisors in his division had not really embraced the team concept. This stance he found shortsighted, for he believed teams were there to stay. As he put it, 'We have no choice but to accept the change' (a statement that would have made Gladis, the instructor, proud). Carlos dismissed managers as 'bunches of, uh, of bourgeois', who likewise dismissed workers as 'people who just work on the floor'.

And, finally, he reiterated his belief in the efficacy of teams, but insisted as well on a commitment from management: 'Well, the idea of teamwork is, you know, very good, but . . . management should give us the tools, the support, encouragement.' Ironically, this discussion begins to show the sort of critical reasoning and consideration of contending perspectives that is at the heart of real learning and education—just the features that, in the last chapter, we saw were missing in training courses at Teamco.

This is an appropriate statement with which to end our case study of Teamco. We are arguing in this book not that the new forms of work associated with the new capitalism are inherently bad but that they are not magic. No silver bullets they, no panaceas. In fact, exaggerated claims about a new work order camouflage the very real struggles that must attend any true reshaping of the organization and social roles of workplaces. The question is whether the reshaping will actually occur, whether corporations will be willing to come face to face with the tensions inherent in any attempt to introduce humanistic, democratic reforms into capitalistic enterprises, and be willing to seek honest ways to address those tensions. Or will corporations put a smiling face on their efforts and pronounce them a success before moving on to the newest quality enhancement program? Our pessimistic prediction is the latter, but we hope this book will help to prompt conversations that will prove us wrong.

6 A tale of one village: global capitalism and Nicaragua

In Chapter 2 we explored fast capitalist ideas in relation to the emergence of the new capitalism and its new work order. We traced some of the dimensions of change in the ways that work is organized, managed, and remunerated. In Chapter 3 we related these changes to the wider theme of 'distributed systems', systems wherein knowledge and control is distributed across many units (people and technology), not pooled at the top. Any full understanding of the new global work order calls for the ability to relate local parts of the emerging global economic system to the global whole. In fact, such 'parts-to-whole reasoning' is celebrated in contemporary ideals and conceptions of learning and knowing in the fast capitalist literature (see Hammer & Champy 1993; Senge 1991). This chapter engages in such reasoning by looking at one local part of the global scene and its very problematic relations to the whole.

Thus far in this book we have, for the most part, concentrated on the so-called developed world. In the last two chapters we looked in detail at one group of new-capitalist workers in the developed world caught in the paradoxes of the new work order. Too often, the so-called undeveloped world, the world of the 'less developed' countries, is but a vague abstraction to those of us in the developed world. We see people in these countries as mere media images, icons of global social and political problems.

In this chapter we will see such people up close, as real individuals trying to participate in the new global economy. Earlier in the book we mentioned that Cardoso (1993) has argued that either less developed countries must enter 'the democratic–technological–scientific race', invest heavily in R & D, and endure the 'information economy' metamorphosis, or become 'unimportant, unexploited, and unexploitable':

> [T]hose countries (or parts thereof) which are unable to repeat the revolution of the contemporary world, and at the same time find a niche in the international market, will end up in the 'worst of all possible worlds'. They will not even be considered worth the trouble of exploitation; they will become inconsequential, of no interest to the developing globalized economy (Cardoso 1993: 156).

Here we will see that it is by no means an easy matter to enter the charmed circle of new-capitalist 'winners'. Many of us know, or believe, that the term 'undeveloped country' bears historical witness to the process by which nations like the United States have actively 'undeveloped' such countries in the drive to 'develop' themselves. We will see, too, that in the new work order people in 'less developed' countries suffer the consequences of being mere parts of complex systems whose centres they are far removed from in time and space.

Our account of fast capitalism recognizes that fast capitalist texts identify some crucial features of contemporary work, and acknowledges their contribution to the framing of future work agendas. At the same time, however, our exploration in Chapter 2 of fast capitalist accounts of the new work order identified a high degree of selectivity and some fatal blind spots. Fast capitalist texts are not inclusive: as we saw 'in theory' in Chapter 2 and 'in practice' in Chapter 4, they leave out important elements of the overall picture of present day work. Most importantly, they fail to consider what the new capitalism means for 'the sinking four-fifths' in modernized economies, and for entire regions of people whose societies are in peril of being locked permanently out of the new world economy.

By virtue of these omissions fast capitalist texts distort the reality they claim to portray, and do so in ways that limit our capacity to anticipate some potentially calamitous problems and to envisage an array of alternative future possibilities. To this extent they work at an ideological level to foreclose or pre-empt a range of potential options, and at a political level to submerge the interests of vast numbers of the world's present and future citizens.

Paradoxically, fast capitalist texts call for enlarged understandings of work, yet they tend to peddle incomplete information and partial pictures of the work world. They call for knowledge workers who can grasp 'wholes' and relate them to 'parts' in complex systems, workers who understand 'the big picture' of their economic contribution to their organizations. When it comes to their own contribution to this ideal, however, we find fast capitalist texts often silent about the full consequences of the new work order—we find that they often frame their issues too narrowly, leaving out cultural, moral, and political aspects in favor of economic ones.

In this chapter we present a case study which delves further into the world of the new capitalism in ways that highlight some of the blind spots in fast capitalist accounts of the new work order and indicate some material consequences of these blind spots. Besides their usefulness as an exercise of negative critique, however, case studies such as this serve a larger and more positive purpose. As Lafontaine (1990, cited in Cardoso 1993: 149) has pointed out, if the old socialist project of the Left is no longer bearing fruit it is because the hour has arrived to build a new one—one that does not live by protest alone, but that may be animated by the utopia of a more just social order. Cardoso argues that when a social project (whether socialism *per se* or more modest projects like critical literacy, critical pedagogy, or critical theory) 'offers mere protest', and even if it attains the status of a 'movement', it will at best 'pave the way for change that [limits] itself to mentalities and ideologies'. It will not serve as 'a political instrument for better days' (ibid: 151).

We believe that in recent years a good deal of critical literacy has developed in ways that preclude its becoming a political instrument for better days, precisely because practices of critical literacy have so often confined themselves to negative critique and modes of textual analysis that fail to advance positive visions and agendas for progressive change. At the very least we need to develop sociocultural approaches to language and literacy that construct as well as deconstruct, that synthesize as well as analyze, that frame ideal 'possible worlds', and that enable readers to unveil textual representations of reality and their interest-serving consequences. The case study that follows is offered in this spirit.

I Square peg in a round hole? The case of San José

Let us consider a seemingly peripheral case. This is a case of contemporary work which would never make it into a fast capitalist text, yet one which speaks more or less directly to the economic reality and circumstances of vast and increasing numbers of people around the world. As such, it is a kind of case that must become more central to our knowledge and understanding of the new work order. Our case study is a light manufacturing cooperative established in the mid-1980s by a group of Nicaraguan peasants, a cooperative named San José.

In 1985 a small group of men and women living in the rural hamlet of Monte Fresco (pop. 1200), 30 kilometers southwest of Managua, agreed to pool their meager financial resources and form a production cooperative. The context was unusual. In 1979 popular opposition forces, galvanized by the Sandinistas, had driven the dictator Somoza from Nicaragua. A new revolutionary government, heavily dominated by members of the Sandinista National Liberation Front, was formed and quickly undertook a range of far-reaching reforms. These included a mass literacy crusade and mass health and vaccination campaigns, official support for a number of 'mass organizations' (e.g., urban and rural workers' unions, a national women's organization), and a number of legal, social, and economic reforms. These initiatives were conceived and implemented within an overall agenda for national development with social justice.

Among the economic innovations were mechanisms and incentives encouraging cooperative approaches to economic production in agriculture and manufacturing. Cooperatives were eligible for a range of incentives and forms of government-sponsored support, including credit advances, price subsidies, and preferential access to raw materials, as well as access to support services designed to assist cooperative enterprises technically, educationally, and administratively.

During the period 1985–88 the San José cooperative grew to include nine men and six women. All had previously experienced insecure, irregular, and poorly paid employment, interspersed with long bouts of unemployment. Most had endured frequent periods of hunger and malnutrition. While many had been better off, strictly speaking, than the lowest stratum of Nicaraguan peasants, others can fairly be said to have lived near the bottom of the Latin American Third World economic heap.

Throughout the life of the cooperative the group (has) stayed clear of loans and other available forms of credit, fearing the loss of whatever they did own in the event of the enterprise failing. They began by producing a simple line of wheat bristle brooms and gradually diversified their product range, providing cleaning utensils for the home: nylon bristle brushes and brooms, toilet brushes, bottle brushes, cotton fiber mop heads (called 'mechas': the kind we associate with wringer mops), and mop handle and clamp mechanisms (called 'lampazos)'.

Before turning to the products and their production, it is important to identify a number of factors tending to favor successful production and a number of factors working against the success of San José. Several positive factors operated during the early years of the cooperative. First, the United States government, beginning with the Reagan administration, became implacably opposed to the Nicaraguan revolution and imposed a crippling economic blockade on the country (as it had done earlier and continues to do against Cuba). The United States government succeeded also in getting other countries to join the blockade. This created a scarcity of imported products in Nicaragua, amplifying local market opportunities for local producers.

At the same time, the Nicaraguan government was eager to preserve whatever it could of its minuscule foreign/hard currency reserves (i.e. dollars) and therefore supported local production in order to minimize imports wherever possible. In this context, San José found itself with positive market opportunities and a viable niche within the local economy. Furthermore, subsidies on basic foodstuffs and other commodities available to cooperatives helped stretch the wages of San José's members, allowing them to plow a good proportion of income back into the enterprise.

The cooperative was established on a small parcel of land owned by the mother of some of the members. Most members lived within 200 meters of the tool shed and factory (although three walked to work from a neighboring community two kilometers away). Several of the group were related by marriage, and all were close friends. There was a high degree of enthusiasm and trust within the group as a whole, all members identifying very closely with the enterprise. They worked long hours. Work itself was characterized by high levels of sociality, camaraderie, and an 'organic' interplay between work and domestic routines.

Since most homes were very close by, younger children could either be left for long periods under the supervision of older children or, during school hours in term time, could be minded 'on the job' as they played in the large factory. Members could leave a work task to get a meal prepared or a child fed, or to tend animals, and drift back into production when the diversion was ended. Work was highly flexible. Hours were recorded, and could be made up at any time. Members settled on production and work schedules that met the dual needs imposed by their personal circumstances and the cooperative's production demands.

A final factor that worked positively in the short run was the serendipitous discovery of San José by international personnel. A doctor taking water samples from wells in the region, at a time when an international project to produce hand pumps for wells was being mooted, became impressed by the industry at San José, then in its second year. This resulted in the cooperative being given a contract to produce the hand-operated pumps in collaboration with the Nicaraguan Engineering University, and receiving machinery, a jeep, and subsequent donations which funded a reliable electricity supply and a high performance lathe.

All these factors make San José sound like a paradigmatic instance of a new-capitalist workplace—ironically, given how 'traditional' it was in many ways. The people constituted a 'community of practice' (see Chapter 3), they distributed their knowledge and work within a flat hierarchy, they avoided having any strong border between their work lives and their private lives, they demonstrated total commitment, and they engaged in flexible and highly adaptive work patterns. Furthermore, they established links to outside providers. This leads one to the view that, in a sense, new-capitalist workplaces try to create high-tech versions of traditional, cooperative, village work settings.

However, a number of negative factors counteracted these positive ones. The negative factors included the low educational level of the workers, a four year period of hyperinflation exacerbated by the economy-sapping effects of the Contra War, and the (consequent) increasingly irregular availability of raw materials, particularly cotton, the basis of mecha production, potentially San José's most sure, enduring, and lucrative product.

Several of the men could neither read nor write. Others, like the coordinator, could read elementary texts but could not write. As children, their labor in the fields had formed an essential part of domestic economies—hence they received minimal (or no) schooling. Most of the women could read and write at a more or less functional level, some of them having managed two or three grades of schooling as children. The cooperative's treasurer, Isabel, had first learned to read and write in the 1980 literacy crusade, and had continued learning to the equivalent of third grade level in the subsequent adult basic education program of voluntary non-formal night study in local neighborhoods. Isabel studied until classes ceased in Monte Fresco.

The hyperinflation peaked in 1989. During a five month period the córdoba became devalued from around 2500 to the US dollar to above 150 000 to the dollar. Not surprisingly, this posed massive administrative and financial challenges to these undereducated producers. It was possible (and happened repeatedly) to make big losses as a result of product price increases not keeping pace with the inflation that occurred between the time of purchase of raw materials and the time that the products were being sold.

The production history of San José presents an interesting and illuminating perspective from which to consider the new capitalism and its fast capitalist representations. The group began by producing a simple line of brooms. The bristles were made from a species of wheat, stitched into shape with wire (using a homemade device of hinged wood, like book covers, that closed to flatten the wheat while it was stitched flat into its permanent shape), and wired to wooden handles that had been rounded laboriously by hand. These 'traditional' brooms were popular and sold well.

A percentage of profits was plowed back into the enterprise to purchase equipment and materials and to increase the scale and range of production. By 1989 production had been diversified. An all-weather concrete block factory had been built, and new machinery included a primitive lathe that would shape one-inch by one-inch timber stakes into wooden handles, a circular saw, arc welder, steel guillotine, electric drill and press, and an array of metal working tools. In addition, the cooperative had obtained a machine that turned nylon pellets into nylon thread under heat.

Production, however, remained labor-intensive, with many products containing handmade components. At the height of production, in 1988–89, the labor-intensive nature of the work meant that, comparatively speaking, the products remained rustic. Mecha, lampazo, and cepillo (brush) production are illustrative. Mecha production began with the unpacking of a large bale of unrefined cotton fiber which had been compressed into the bale. The women would draw out strands of fiber and pull them tight, using the full length of the factory floor (about 60 feet). The strands were then wound around two nails some 24 inches apart and cut with a machete. This left 24-inch lengths of cotton fiber—by the ton! These were kept orderly and gathered into lots weighing one pound (using scales). The principle was one pound of cotton per mecha. Each pound of cotton was laid out evenly in 6-inch widths, and was held together by a calico ribbon sewn flat through the middle of the cotton; that is, 12 inches in from each end.

These hanks of cotton were then taken to a rectangular frame built like a table without its top. Women (mainly) and children sat around the frame on stools or forms. The hanks of cotton were tossed over the frame with the ribbon atop the frame, so that one side of the hank fell down the outside of the frame towards the seated person's lap. The worker then took several strands of fiber and rubbed them between the palms of her hands with an action that plaited the strands into a twist that stayed together. She then repeated this exercise all the way across the first half of the hank, resulting in 15–20 plaits of more or less equal 'body'. The hank was then flipped over the other way and the remaining side plaited.

The completed mechas were tossed on to a table. One worker (usually Gilberto or Jorge, men in their twenties) would inspect each mecha for evenness, give it a shake to get rid of loose fibers, and then put it into a plastic bag and heat-seal the open end of the bag with a primitive model of heat sealer (electrical wiring everywhere!).

Lampazo and nylon brush production were similarly labor-intensive. To hold the mechas securely, lampazos required nuts and bolts, as well as various types of brackets and movable parts, all of which cooperative members produced themselves. Nylon brush and broom products involved additional processes. For example, the bristles were made by producing nylon thread from pellets under heat. The threads were wound on to a homemade mechanism similar to a garden-hose reel, and then bundled like rope and taken to the factory. There one of the men, usually Gilberto, would cut bristles to length using a large pair of scissors. A cluster of bristles, more or less the same number, judged quickly by eye, would be held together by a twist of wire in the middle of the cluster put on with a pair of pliers.

Gilberto would make literally hundreds of bristle clusters while others were producing the brush or broom bodies outside the factory. When the bodies were delivered, Gilberto, or one or more of the youths or younger children, would grab a bristle cluster, poke the wire twist into a hole, then punch the wire to the bottom of the hole using a hammer and punch. The process was completed for each hole and each cluster of bristles. A small brush for scrub-washing clothes might contain 30 holes, a broom head as many as 50. Bristles were produced in different gauges for different types of product. Different color dyes were put into the pellets to make mulish-colored bristle combinations— to lend products an aesthetic dimension. (Rolando was typically in charge of the 'aesthetics'.) With the bristles punched into the bodies, Gilberto would trim them off using scissors.

The products, as one would expect, were never entirely precise. Nonetheless, within these broad parameters of production San José's workers pursued constant innovation, continual improvement, and higher quality as 'organic' principles. To take one very simple example, initially the mechas were not bagged. They were simply bundled together in lots of a dozen for buyers to purchase at the factory for resale in markets. In response to what they saw as the 'more professional' finish of competitors who did bag their mechas, the San José people renovated a primitive heat-sealing tool and hooked it up to the electric current.

Many further examples could be provided of San José's workers trying to maximize market share through quality control and adaptive improvements. These were, of course, proportionate to the level of technology being employed and the degree of labor intensity involved in the production processes. It is one thing to take great care in trimming bristles with scissors but another thing altogether to have machines that cut bristles to length in the first place and trim them at the end of the process.

Bearing in mind that production remained highly labor-intensive, the scale and efficiency of activity were impressive. Vendors from city markets collected lampazos in lots of 500. On a good day 450 or more mechas, a lucrative product, were produced and bagged. Most families associated with San José had built permanent-material dwellings from income, purchasing materials as they could afford them and commencing construction once all the necessities had been acquired. These homes stood out in the wider community in terms of size, quality, and amenities. The children were all in school, the older ones attending the 'colegio' in Managua. Most intended to continue on to university or other tertiary institutions.

Such factors indicated a quite remarkable change in life quality over a five year period. By the same token, the very success represented by this scale of production contained the seeds of demise. By 1989 the cooperative's level of production and commercial exchange, and the hyperinflation that gripped and bled the national economy, meant that the demands of administering and managing the enterprise far outstripped the members' capacities. However, immediate assistance was seemingly at hand. The Support Office for Small Enterprises, established by the government to help cooperative producers, came to offer a week-long seminar on basic business administration and accountancy.

The content and pedagogy of the seminar were designed precisely for people like Isabel, building on existing knowledge, experience, and print skills in order to bring about new understanding and competency. Isabel testified to the effectiveness of the seminar and the possibilities it opened up for San José:

When we were in a group the ones who understood would help me and
explain how the income and expenditure worked; how the balance sheet
is done; how you find out if the cooperative is losing money or has a
profit. I found out what things were important for the cooperative or
were damaging. I realized that here [San José] we sometimes do things
that are making a loss and we carry on anyway. I learned how to do
the accounts and the balance, to keep the bank book, how to see the
expenditure and income figures, all of that. For me this was important
to learn because I didn't understand it before but it's my job. This
seminar was very important for me . . . I've started to check our bank
account. I was able to do that. One day I sat down to do it—what I
learned in the seminar—and I did it well (interview, October 1989).

It is common knowledge that the Sandinista government was
defeated in the February 1990 elections. The new government removed
import restrictions, moving quickly toward a free market economy. The
United States government lifted the economic blockade with equal
haste. These changes, not surprisingly, impacted strongly on San José's
activity. The Nicaraguan consumer market was opened to imported lines
that were cheaper and perceived to be of higher quality than local
variants. This was a classic example of the 'local' being driven out by
the 'global'.

San José's nylon brushes and brooms were early casualties, followed quickly by lampazos. San José's coordinator, Pedro, summed up
the situation retrospectively and diagnosed the cooperative's future
prospects with characteristic candor:

What is handmade is not valued, and that's why we can't be
competitive with a free market—it's impossible to compete with a
machine-made product. The products from other countries are cheaper
than ours in Nicaragua—which are of lower quality because of the lack
of resources to improve a product. That's why our cooperative is not
active now—we are unable to compete. After 1989 Nicaragua started
again to import products from other countries, like El Salvador—in
particular, products that we produced. Theirs were cheaper. We started
to industrialize the production of our mecha, and the handles, but then
the factory that produced the timber closed down, and also the factory
that produced the cotton. So the problem with industrializing the
mecha—which has a good market—is partly that the local factories
providing raw materials closed down, and partly the cost of getting raw
materials from other countries. It's expensive. We thought about loans,
but that's not a good idea. We really just need raw materials because
we have the electricity and we have the machines. We need raw
materials, and some money to buy them. We invested our money in

building the factory and the storerooms for our products. When higher prices for raw materials came we couldn't do anything. The money we got we invested. All you see here—the factory, the machines—are due to our efforts. All we made we invested in this factory—we never thought we would close down (interview, February 1995).

While mechas remained a viable proposition, cotton supplies became increasingly irregular and expensive. During 1991 and 1992 cotton supply was absolutely minimal, with gaps of 2–5 months between small supplies, which were never sufficient to provide more than a week or two of work anyway. In fact, by January 1992 the major income-earning activities of 1989 had virtually disappeared.

Production was restricted to two lines. First, a sophisticated imported lathe was being used to convert rough-sawn timber stakes into high quality handles (bolillos) for brooms and mops. Profits on this line were good, although the local market was finite. Handles sold for twice the cost of the timber. The machine could, however, with the unskilled labor of one person, produce more in a day than might be sold in a month.

The other line was especially interesting. The cooperative had returned to where it began, producing wheat bristled brooms of the original design for which there remained a traditional market. Cooperative members were using land to grow the appropriate species of wheat, rather than cropping yuca, trigo (sorghum), rice, and maize, as they had in 1989. The original homemade machines, built in 1984 for shaping and holding bristles and for unwinding the wire for stitching, were in use again. In stunning juxtaposition the imported lathe provided the technological complement, furnishing high quality handles for these homely brooms.

The women, then, were all effectively out of paid work and almost all had retired to their homes. The men were on severely reduced work schedules. At least two men had left the cooperative: one to produce charcoal for sale in the city; the other to clean warehouses in another country. During 1993 and 1994 the men increasingly sought seasonal work, odd jobs calling for skills and tools they had acquired during the cooperative's good years, or, in the case of one man, a city job as a security guard for a supermarket. The youngest man entered training for the priesthood.

Despite these setbacks hope lived on and, with it, interest in innovation and continuous improvement driven by the dream of a return to previous levels of activity. Early in 1994 the cooperative was contracted to produce 13 000 bolillos (handles). This, however, amounted to just a few days of highly repetitive labor for a solitary male worker, pushing timber stakes through the high performance lathe.

This coincided with a small supply of cotton, enough to provide an opportunity for San José to move its quality agenda for mecha production a quantum step forward. This time the cotton came as refined thread on large spools, not in the large bales of unspun fiber. Plaiting had gone as a production process. Instead, several spools were set at one end of the factory, and thread from each was drawn to the other end and connected up to an electric hand-held drill. The drill was held like a pistol, toward the spools, and the trigger pressed, twisting the threads of cotton into compact regular twists. These twists of several strands of cotton, each corresponding to a single handmade plait in the original process, were wound around a revolving purpose-built steel frame, and cut to length. A pound of such plaits were then sewn together on an industrial sewing machine, using calico ribbon as before—producing a mecha.

This highly inventive approach was much more precise than the old hand-plaiting approach, and much less labor-intensive. The plaiting frame was gone. Production rates were higher and the product was (in some senses) of a higher quality. Only three people, however, were required to produce what ten or more had previously been engaged in: only better. The factory was no longer a bustling lively social scene—just three people, one electric drill, five or so spools, a rotating steel frame, a sewing machine, and the redoubtable heat sealer.

During 1994, and having seemingly located a more reliable and regular supply of good cotton, San José took a further bold step toward enhanced quality production of mechas. The group purchased, for $US1200, from a factory that was closing down, a machine used to mass produce high precision plaits for mechas. The decision to take this step was made explicitly in the interests of increasing market share by increasing quality. In the coordinator's words:

> We need always to sit down and work out how to produce more appropriately and to win a market by achieving a better finish. In the case of mechas we were doing a good job and could compete with the El Salvadoreans because our product was good quality. The Salvadorean mechas contained dust. Ours didn't. When we got the cotton to make the mechas we used good cotton to make them dust-free. The dusty ones are not good. Ours are whiter. They look better (interview, 18 February 1995).

While this initiative made excellent sense in principle, in practice it has been a dismal failure to date. The cost of purchasing the machine—small though it seems to be relative to our sense of business finance—left the cooperative with strictly limited capital for buying raw materials. Even so, there was enough in reserve to allow for small quantity purchases on the local market, with the chance to gradually accumulate profits. One local factory produced good quality cotton at a price that allowed San José to be competitive. This factory, however, failed financially and was forced to close, after providing just two small supplies of raw cotton to San José.

It was the only local source of supply, meaning that the cooperative was forced to look for suppliers outside Nicaragua. This, of course, increased the price and put the price of cotton effectively beyond the cooperative's reach. Hence, after just two short runs, the machine was forced into premature retirement. By February 1995 it had lain idle for several months.

The other potential earner was bolillos. San José's high performance lathe produced high quality handles: smooth, with a shiny surface; of exportable quality. The machine could produce up to 10 000 units per day, attended by one worker. Noél, one of San José's younger members, explained how the productive and profitable use of this costly investment was also thwarted:

> We had an export market for bolillos. We found a channel to export to Mexico, but we couldn't produce because we couldn't get raw materials. The timber factory closed. There is timber in Nicaragua, but there is now a law against milling it. This is for conservation. We had the machine to make the bolillos, but we couldn't get the wood. So we lost the contract. In earlier times, Honduras, for example, didn't have timber to make bolillos, because of the need for conservation. But Nicaragua was still milling timber. Then the thing that happened to other countries started to happen to us. No raw materials! (interview, 16 February 1995.)

During February 1995 only two, strictly short-term, earning activities were in evidence at San José. Both were individual subsistence efforts and hence contributed nothing to the cooperative. One of the men had planted a crop of wheat the previous season: the species of wheat used for making brooms. For the third successive year there had been poor rains and his crop was minute. He had enough wheat to make just 15 dozen brooms, at 5 córdobas per unit (6.6 córdobas equalled $US1 at the time). There were enough wooden stakes left over from the previous year to make handles on the lathe. Even allowing the handles as a cost-free component, this man's total crop production yielded less than two days of work and $140 worth of product.

In the second activity another of the men had a contract to produce eighty folding wooden chairs for sale to a church. He cut down a laurel tree in the forest and brought it back to the factory piece by piece in a wheelbarrow. The timber was reduced to size with absolutely minimum waste, using the powerful circular saw and a joinery attachment that thicknessed the timber accurately. Any scraps of wood were used to fire the family's cooking oven.

The San José cooperative still exists in principle. But there is pessimism about the future, plus pressure from some of the members to sell the machinery and divide up the proceeds. Isabel explained that 'because we are doing nothing we decided to sell the machinery. If we are not using it, it will deteriorate. It is very sad to have to sell what means so much to us—sad to think that everything has to go'. In reply to the question of whether the cooperative had a future, Isabel felt obliged to say:

> No, because there's not . . . like me . . . we don't have the energy,
> the enthusiasm we used to have—for example, the factory has
> closed many times but because of our enthusiasm we used to find
> solutions and start up again. But now we don't have the enthusiasm
> we used to have and the men are working in other places. And
> that's why I feel there's no future (interview, 18 February 1995).

Pedro, the coordinator, insisted that viable markets for the cooperative's products still existed. He said: 'There are markets for bolillos, brooms, lampazos and mechas. There's enough market for work, but we don't have raw materials.' He identified possibilities for getting the factory back into production:

> Asking for a loan, but we don't like to ask for a loan. We have to
> be very careful, because loans are things that can take you down.
> As a membership we don't want to do that. There are other things
> as well. The way banks lend you money—it's a matter of having an
> export contract with a client, and a guaranteed amount of work that
> will bring money into Nicaragua. The process of getting clients
> takes several steps. First, you need a contract with those who
> provide raw materials. Second, the people who are going to buy the
> product. Third, in order to make this contract serious we have to be
> sure that everyone is going to be doing their part well. For people
> like us it is very difficult to arrange all these things (interview, 18
> February 1995).

Like Isabel, Pedro didn't see much future prospect for the co-operative early in 1995. He explained:

> In Cándida's house, she doesn't work now, but her son Alexis is maintaining her. Santiago is working in Managua to maintain the house. Luisa isn't really getting by. She's making hand bread to sell in the neighborhood, but it's not enough. She's surviving because God wants her to survive. If you're not working you're not getting money. Everyone is struggling to survive. Some of the members want to sell the machines, because we have nothing to work on with the machines. But some of the women who worked here, for example Luisa, if you asked her she would say 'don't sell the machines'; but the others don't see any way out, and neither do I. If we improve our products, as we have and can, we can get into the market. But for that we need money. For example, the brooms that Jorge makes, they are everywhere. They're good for selling (interview, 18 February 1995).

Each family was managing to survive, by one means or another. But, from an ethical perspective, the cost was high in important ways. Santiago, the illiterate refiner of rope pump components and former 'lecturer' to fellow campesinos in the 'university' on matters of component design, worked as a security guard six and a half days a week in a city supermarket, leaving each morning at 5.30 by bus and arriving back after 8.00 each night. Gilberto, also illiterate, was eking out a living cutting firewood by machete for sale locally. Edmundo also worked at times in firewood and charcoal production (as did Reinaldo, who had left the cooperative to work for himself). Pedro and Noél worked irregularly in carpentry and joinery; some of that work, too, meant using local timber resources. Rolando, illiterate refiner of lampazos and 'color coordinator' for nylon brush and broom bristles, cut sugar cane by machete during the season, and raised some cattle with assistance from his wife's family. The women were confined to unpaid household work.

In September 1995 a Dutch development worker living in a neighboring community reported that a sign on the main highway at the entrance to a lane leading to the cooperative announced that the factory and its machinery were up for sale.

The situation reflects an unacceptable level of wasted human capacities. Besides the waste of Isabel's learning, Santiago's capacity to refine, and other skills evident among the cooperative members, is the fact that some of the older children were now obliged to work for youth rates in city supermarkets in order to help maintain their families. Dulce and Erica worked full time in this capacity. Erica, top of her class in

1989, with the world seemingly in front of her, stacked foodstuffs eight hours daily. Alexis worked seven-hour shifts during the week, supporting his mother and siblings, and then began his daily studies for university. He said the work took the edge off his energy for studying.

In addition to the cost in terms of wasted human capacities and hardwon skills, the ecological cost is enormous. At least five of the nine male members were depending on timber from nearby forests for their livelihood. The local forest was being stripped at an incredible rate, quite apart from former milling activity, and clear signs of 'desertification' were in evidence.

II What to make of San José?

The members of the San José cooperative organized themselves in ways that are quite like those suggested by fast capitalist texts. They were well aware of the forces of competition in the new global capitalism and of the need for 'quality'. Nonetheless, they failed. In fact, their attempts at quality and competitiveness through technology served both to reduce the distinctive localness of their products and to drive a number of the cooperative's members back into menial work and poverty. This immiseration of a large number of people as against a few 'enchanted' and 'empowered' workers seems to be, as we pointed out in Chapter 2, a hallmark of the new global capitalism.

What are we to make of San José, then? Where do these people and their enterprise fit into the new capitalism and the new work order? Or, to push the issue further, where do their peers—the illiterate, semiliterate, and otherwise undereducated landless rural laborers of Monte Fresco; the peasant smallholders on marginal land anywhere in the world; the vast masses of marginal urban dwellers throughout the underdeveloped world—fit in? What are the implications for fast capitalist accounts of the new work order?

Just as the case study in Chapters 4 and 5 did in the United States context, the example of San José cautions us to look closely at fast capitalist accounts of successful work and business. At one level, fast capitalist texts advance sets of principles, rules, and criteria for 'getting it right'. If these are read as sufficient conditions for success that apply widely or generally, we are in for some major disappointments. Even if they are read only as necessary conditions, providing the basis for getting into a competitive situation and not necessarily sufficient for success, many 'triers' are still likely to be disappointed if they fail to take into account the sheer differences in the baselines from which enterprises in different locations set out.

It wasn't the 'micro-setting' of work relations, attitudes, and organization—so heavily pushed by fast capitalist texts—that undid San José. This they got right. Although they had not read the books, they can be construed as having followed all the right fast capitalist advice. The members of the cooperative thought about processes, not isolated tasks; they engaged in flexible production; they adopted technology; they engaged in both 'incremental improvement' and 'radical change'. They asked the tough questions: 'Why are we doing this at all?'; 'Why not think of doing or producing something else altogether?'; 'What's our real business?'. They engaged in 'flat structures', 'shared collective responsibility', 'every worker a decision-maker', and 'worker empowerment'; they had high motivation, full commitment and loyalty, and full identification with 'the mission', 'core values', and 'vision' of the enterprise. In other words, we can construe them as a 'textbook case' of fast capitalist methods.

What undid San José was not the 'micro-setting', the small frame to which fast capitalist texts pay most of their attention. Rather, it was the bigger picture—the larger frame—of global and nation-state politics, historical exploitation, access to information and education, the complex workings of technology, and the winner-take-all nature of contemporary capitalism.

Of course, fast capitalists have a whole gamut of response options for handling cases like San José. These range from the fact that their writings have not been directed at 'undeveloped' economies to the claim that they presuppose particular levels of knowledge, technology and expertise. This, however, is precisely the point. Fast capitalists have left the wider social and geopolitical context out of their accounts and their 'vision'. It matters little whether this is by ideological design, or because it is of no direct concern to them or their intended audience, or whether it is simply by omission, myopically. When we do take the wider context into account we are forced to recognize that it makes for winners and losers in thoroughly predictable ways. In this respect the new capitalism is not really new—it is just an acceleration and a heightening of the effects of the old capitalism.

To appreciate what this means for people like San José's members, not to mention the millions of citizens in even poorer countries who are considerably worse off than they are, we need to pay close attention to such matters as the new international division of labor, the conditions for success of national, regional, and local economies under the new globalism, and the historical circumstances and traditions of particular nations and groups (e.g. whether they are former client states, have dependent colonial or neocolonial histories, have high foreign debt and low technology levels, and endure large price differentials between exports and imports). Upon closer examination we find that, ultimately, what counts against a San José far outweighs what it has going for it.

To give these issues the attention they deserve calls for much greater depth and detail than can be provided here. The main contours, however, are clear enough. San José, like Nicaraguan enterprise in general, was operating from a very low technological base. The infrastructure available to them could not possibly deliver 'high quality' lampazos, although it could deliver (acceptably) high quality bolillos and mechas. Having met the necessary conditions (good quality and low price) for competitiveness in these areas, however, San José tripped over on the combination of finite local markets and insufficient knowledge and education.

The local bolillo market was strictly finite; and members lacked the skills, knowledge, and other resources needed both to identify and secure export markets, and to deal with such markets and their entrepreneurs. Worse still, they lacked even the basic knowledge and competencies needed to administer their (at times considerable) successes in ways that ensured profitability and maintained sufficient capital to purchase raw materials that would keep the machines and workers in operation.

Beyond these stumbling blocks lay other traps originating from historical legacies and circumstances. Progressive laws—indeed, pragmatically and ethically necessary laws—designed to limit further local deforestation effectively put San José legally out of the bolillo market, for want of competitively priced timber. A combination of factors—including low world prices for commodities like cotton, the decline of agricultural production generally in Nicaragua resulting from the flight to exile of many experienced large landowners and administrators during the Sandinista period, and problems of economic management within the agricultural sector—militated against local cotton production, to the point that supplier factories were going out of business.

Other potential niche markets (e.g. furniture and crafts) were already saturated.

San José's dilemma reflects the strictly limited capacity of Nicaraguan governments and relevant institutions to provide the kind and degree of steerage and other enabling conditions that would expand markets abroad, to develop effective development strategies in the face of powerful historical and political impediments, and to increase tourism—which would bring additional markets for portable products into Nicaragua, thereby augmenting export drives. To a large extent these limitations bespeak colonial and neocolonial traditions of dependent underdevelopment (e.g. Frank 1967; Galeano 1973; Vilas 1989), client statehood (Carnoy and Samoff 1990), and a centuries-old legacy of obscene price differentials between commodities extracted or produced locally, (typically under externally imposed dictates from the colonial (Spain) and neocolonial (United States) controlling powers) and imported products sold back to Nicaragua by these same controlling powers, and under similar duress.

In these historical conditions infrastructural and educational development was always constrained, in accordance with the interests of the more powerful 'partners'.

The larger background of Nicaragua sketched here is by no means unique. It is, in one form or another, one set of details or another, the narrative of the Third World. The alarming thing is that Nicaragua is by no means at the bottom of the heap, although it is certainly very badly off. The case of San José and its immediate social and geopolitical context points squarely to the issue of North–South relations within the 'global village' (see Cardoso 1993), as well as to Zygmunt Bauman's concern that for people in countries like Nicaragua 'development' means—as it has hitherto meant for them—developing 'the dependency of men and women on things and events they can neither produce, control, see nor understand' (Bauman 1995: 30–31).

While 'complex distributed systems' are all the rage among academics and in the new capitalism, as we saw in Chapter 3, the members of the San José cooperative are the victims of a complex system that operates to the advantage of others. These others had already loaded the deck during the old capitalism's heyday. The new capitalism's complex global systems further operate to drive large numbers of people into misery comparable to the worst excesses of the beginnings of industrial capitalism—even amid the high-tech successes of an enchanted few. But talk of complex systems and global competition—even of new capitalism—effaces the moral responsibility for the past and moral obligations for the present of the 'winners' in both the old and the new capitalism. 'Competition' implies that the game is fair. But it is no such thing.

III Critical literacy and the Fourth World

If we are to move beyond critique to imagine new, more just worlds, we will have to change both our talk and our perspectives. We saw in Chapter 2 that fast capitalist literature is prone to a form of consumer determinism: the changes in our societies and throughout the world are due to the demands for quality on the part of 'informed' customers in a globalized free market. If there is pain and suffering, then it's no one's fault—just the workings of the market.

Such talk effaces the responsibilities of elites in the developed countries, and effaces *our* responsibilities as citizens, by narrowing the frame to exclude moral, social, and geopolitical issues. The customers who fuel the new capitalism (on the fast capitalist account) are *us*. We can start our resistance by flatly refusing to see ourselves primarily as consumers driven by the complex systems of global markets, and, rather, seeing ourselves as moral agents with a new globalized citizenship. In a complex system, events on the periphery redound to massively affect the system's center. Today's world is a complex system and *we* will, indeed, ultimately pay the price for the failure of San José and similar failures in Third World pockets of our own developed countries. We will pay the price through violence and chaos. If one is not convinced by humanitarian arguments, then one can be assured that social justice is fast becoming a matter of quality of life, economic necessity, and indeed survival, for all of us.

'The true revolution of our century', Cardoso (1993) argues, is 'the marriage of science, technology and freedom' (154). The 'freedom' he refers to is the freedom associated with the sorts of decentralized, low hierarchy systems we talked about in Chapter 3. It is a freedom that Mikhail Gorbachev instigated with glasnost, that paved the way to breaking down the East–West divide, making the East more admissible to 'free' markets. It is, likewise, a freedom represented in the increased prominence of social movements and devolved responsibility to communities within the contemporary political arena, where political activity is freed up from domination by parties and centrist states. Finally, it is a freedom that is evident in new-capitalist organizations where the hierarchy and locus of control have become flatter and more dispersed. This kind of freedom, then, is based on a recognition 'that "centralism", of whatever stripe, undermines creativity and hinders technical progress' (152).

While science and technology certainly fuelled the old capitalism, they have recently become wedded, as Cardoso argues, to this freedom of distributed, decentralized systems. This, says Cardoso, can be conceived as a marriage of university (= science, theory), enterprise (= new technologies under new-style management and new corporate visions or missions), and public authority (= decentralized political forms, devolution, social movements).

But while this freedom—like talk of global competition and distributed systems—decenters control, it removes any real sense of human agency. Human misery becomes a mere by-product of complex necessity, indeed even 'progress', since this sort of freedom appears to be (and is, in part) a 'good'. However, theorists like Castells (1993) and Cardoso reveal an international division of labor characterized by vast inequalities—to the point, it will be recalled, of possible exclusion of entire national and even continental economies from the new world economy. The theory-driven, value-added, information-based global economy has ushered in an international division of labor reflecting primarily 'the capacity to create new knowledge and apply it rapidly, via information processing and telecommunications, to a wide range of human activities in ever broadening space and time' (Carnoy et al. 1993: 6).

Castells argues that the notion of the Third World as an identifiable entity no longer exists. The fundamental features of the new work order, and the factors influencing success and failure, identified by Castells, have splintered Third World economies into four groups:

- Clear winners: the Asian newly industrializing countries
- Potential winners: e.g. Mexico (with access to NAFTA) and Brazil
- China and India (with potentially vast markets and abundant high-skilled/value-adding/symbolic-analytic 'human capital')
- Clear losers: the 'Fourth World' of marginal rural economies and sprawling urban peripheries (many located in Africa and Latin America).

What has changed fundamentally for the Fourth World is that it has become possible for vast tracts of humanity to be dismissed now as simply having nothing of relevance to contribute to the new world economy—if we insist, that is, on seeing relevance as 'added value' through knowledge and technology in the name of 'quality'. Fertile land, cheap unskilled labor, and mineral resources, in a post-industrial information economy, are no longer at the premium of earlier times. This is a qualitative change of massive significance.

The 'revolutionary marriage' of science, technology, and freedom has crystallized a vast Fourth World. The marriage, being not simply economic (science/technology) but political (social systems/freedom) as well, means that to be admissible to 'the globe'—to join the contemporary revolution—Fourth World nations need to construct new kinds of societies (post-totalitarian, post-dictatorial, post-feudal, post-tribal), as well as develop new economically enabling infrastructures. The question of whether this is possible, and if so how, must take account, as our case study of Nicaragua has argued, of history and of the ongoing perpetuation of history reflected within the very foundations of the new capitalism itself.

These nations necessarily cannot achieve an integration into the new world order unless there occurs a radical change in the *rules of the game*. The beginnings of changing the rules is to refuse to believe that they are simply a matter of necessities beyond our ken or control, as so much of the fast capitalist literature implies. We certainly do not have to believe and act as if 'quality' as defined by technology is the litmus test of what to buy and consume, let alone of the 'good life'. A brightly colored brush from the San José cooperative could have stood for much more than a good buy if only we citizens of the globe had a good enough 'education'—that is, one that showed us clearly the larger frame around issues (including the production and use of brushes) that fast capitalists want us to see as merely economic or lifestyle issues. The beginning of changing the rules can be, as well, the refusal to take for granted the meanings of words in the new capitalism—to begin to see that 'global competition' can sometimes mean global exploitation, that 'worker empowerment' and 'flat hierarchies' can sometimes mean high-touch and high-tech control, that 'freedom' has many meanings in different contexts and that people are not free if 'empowered' in a system whose effects they cannot ward off, that 'decentralization' and 'distributed control' can sometimes hide the sources of exploitation, control, and power, as well as the workings of history.

We are arguing, then, throughout this book, that the words and deeds of the new capitalism—for instance, the words and deeds of fast capitalists and their texts—ought to become a central focus of critical literacy. We saw in Chapter 1 that a sociocultural approach to literacy takes the view that language must always be understood in its social, cultural, historical, and political *contexts*. We are arguing here that one of these contexts, crucial in our 'new times', is the context of the new work order in all its ramifications. Language, indeed our very humanity, is in danger of losing meaning if we do not carefully reflect on this context and its attempts to make *us* into new kinds of people: for example, people who are 'smart' because they buy the highest 'quality' brushes—but do not care about, or even see, the legacies of their greed and ignorance writ large on the world.

The symptomatic problems of the 'South' remain generically the same as they have been throughout the twentieth century: poverty, hunger, illiteracy, 'backwardness'. It is important to recognize that these are still the basic problems (problems the world community has tried, one way or another, to address during modernity) if politically progressive people are not to be overwhelmed by a sense of futility, and yield to the belief that the South simply cannot be brought into the fold, cannot be integrated.

The burgeoning awareness of globalization among modern ('advantaged') populations, and the growing pressure to think of ourselves as members of a global community, are of a piece with the central clue to addressing the challenge of the emerging Fourth World: namely, identifying these problems of poverty, hunger, dispossession, poor health, undereducation, and chronic defeat as matters to be tackled at the global level. This recognition, Cardoso (1993) argues, is tantamount to embracing a 'new humanism'. This is an ethical perspective that 'owns' the humanity of all those beset by the legacies of dependence and deprivation, a humanity that risks being lost when people merit recognition only as 'consumers' or 'value adders'.

At the same time, this perspective recognizes that in different regions and societies the short and medium term approaches required of the global community in order to preserve hope and to pursue long term integration will vary significantly:

> The . . . 'new humanism' may mean, for many countries, something like: renegotiation of the foreign debt in terms compatible with development, plus technology transfer, plus access to world markets. For other countries it may mean nothing less than the direct transfer of food, health care, and schooling. (Cardoso 1993: 159).

Rebuilding a progressive vision within the broad critical tradition of social democracy begins, on this view, with identifying the problems of the South as proper objects for a concerted global approach, just as problems of ecology and environment are being seen as surmountable through global action. Ecological and environmental degradation is by no means an object of mere critique. Rather, concerns here have been transformed into full-fledged social praxis. Positive visions of sustainability and regeneration have been framed, and positive action within the public sphere—including formal education—is actively fomented around these visions. Formal and non-formal educational activity alike, pound out messages and agendas of civic responsibility and enlist learner–citizens in actions which shape ecological and environmental consciousness in the process of ministering to the natural world.

The situation is very different, however, when it comes to critique of economic practices and articulating positive visions for the economic order. Educators typically feel compelled here to confine their conceptions and practices of critical literacy or critical pedagogy at most to formal analysis and deconstruction of texts—stopping short, even, of calling for the textual production of positive economic visions, let alone their incorporation into any kind of embodied praxis. Yet effective critique presupposes some positive vision. The analysis and argument presented in this book bespeak the urgency of effective critical engagement with the new capitalism and its new global work order. The positive vision needed to augment critical literacy directed at the economic practices of daily life begins with an ethical commitment at two levels.

The first is a commitment to acting on the principle that promoting good and minimizing harm to human beings is our primary obligation as moral agents. Hence, while we have—undeniably—an ethical obligation to nurture and restore the natural environment, we have an even more pressing ethical obligation to nurture human life and ameliorate human degradation. If informed ecological and environmental concerns are appropriate catalysts for envisioning positive ideals and enlisting embodied commitment via education, so much more must be informed concerns revealed by investigations of the new work order. Unless we embrace this level of commitment, we cannot consistently claim the status or entitlements of moral beings.

The second level of ethical commitment is a corollary of the first. If we are to build a global *community* in which the interests and well-being of all become the concern of all—which, after all, is what it means to *be* a community—we must ensure that learning is framed in ways that promote a practical commitment to identifying human harm and degradation where it occurs, and to acting in ways that address and overcome it. This is a call to undertake education as a moral engagement which is practical as well as intellectual or formal. It requires the disposition to seek, articulate, and act upon positive visions which are always acknowledged as provisional and open to revision in the light of evidence and critique.

As Cardoso's work makes clear, the broad content of a positive vision from which to mount effective critique of the new capitalism and its new work order, and by which to transcend merely negative critique, is no mystery. It is simply a matter of 'naming' it, 'owning' it, and carrying it into our critical practice. And this naming means adopting the widest frames possible. Ironically, one way to do this, we believe, is to tell stories like our story of San José. Then the 'global' becomes real people with very real sophistication involved in very real struggles of which we are most certainly a part. Our argument in this book implies that critical educators have a responsibilty to frame economic and other 'new-capitalist' issues in the broad context of what it means to be human, and to be a member of an economically and humanly sustainable global community that does not obliterate local differences.

7 What is to be done?

We have reached the end of our book. In earlier chapters we have identified and explored complexities and paradoxes for which we believe there are not easy answers. Along the way we have modelled and explained an array of sociocultural tools, concepts, perspectives, and frames of mind which, we believe, are helpful—though by no means the *only* useful possibilities—for others concerned with exploring and addressing the complexities and paradoxes of the new work order. We will revisit these tools, concepts, perspectives, and frames of mind in this final chapter, in a calm of reflection following the turbulence of our case studies. We cannot offer any definitive solutions, and do not pretend to do so. Rather, we recognise that there is a dire need for renewed thought, critique, and struggle. Having arrived at the end, we leave you with an analysis, a range of analytic, conceptual and critical tools, and our own initial attempt to explore directions we believe are vital in the quest to frame and pursue viable futures.

1 The new work order

In newspapers and on television we hear about the forces and consequences of the new capitalism nearly every day. For example, on 5 September 1995—Labor Day in the United States—Scott Leigh wrote in the *Boston Globe* that this federal holiday, established 101 years ago to celebrate working people, had increasingly taken on 'the mournful aspect of a surrender ceremony'. Though the United States' economy had returned to better health after several years of recession, economic data from a recent study showed that having shared the struggles of their employers through the tough years of recession, American workers were not receiving 'a proportionate piece of the benefit' which followed the upturn. While a 'profit-powered bull market' stampeded to new heights, real wages were slumping 'like a gored matador'. An EIP macroeconomist, Dean Baker, cited evidence from the study that a major shift in power had occurred within workplaces, 'from labour to capital'. The twin trends of escalating inequality in the workplace and a transfer of profit 'from workers to corporations' had produced a declining living standard for most workers (*Boston Globe*, 5 September 1995, Focus Section, pp.65, 69).

The same issue of the *Globe* contained an editorial column that claims:

> The sagging of millions of middle-class Americans back into working-class status, and the drop of millions of working-class people into the welfare class, is probably the single greatest force loose in the political system today. It partially explains all manner of hostilities playing havoc with civic comity: resentments based on race, affirmative action, immigrant status, welfare and government set-asides for this category or that age group (David Nyhan, 'The laying off and laying out of the working stiff', p.68).

A month later, on 4 October, the *Globe* ran an article, headlined 'France's interior minister warns of unrest if economy isn't righted'. The article reported the French Industry Minister, Yves Galland, as saying that France could face social upheaval on the scale of the May 1968 riots if problems of poverty and unemployment were not solved. Speaking to bankers at an investment conference, the Minister claimed that French society was on the very brink of 'incomprehension' and 'refusal'. If precautions were not taken, he said, 'serious tension' such as France experienced in 1968 could occur. Yet, whilst accepting that France was experiencing 'a social fracture' and 'an employment problem', Minister Galland claimed that industrial restructuring was essential to restore competitiveness and generate employment (p.16).

So much, then, for the workers. What about the managers? Here's what Andy Grove, the CEO of Intel Corp (which had sales of $11.5 billion in 1994) has to say to managers:

> You have no choice but to operate in a world shaped by globalization and the information revolution. There are two options: adapt or die. The new environment dictates two rules: first, everything happens faster; second, anything that can be done will be done, if not by you, then by someone else, somewhere. Let there be no misunderstanding: these changes lead to a less kind, less gentle, and less predictable workplace . . .

> In principle, every hour of your day should be spent increasing
> the output or the value of the output of the people for whom you
> are responsible (*Fortune*, 18 September 1995, pp. 229–30).

Of course, the 'morality' that Grove expresses—if you don't do it
someone else will; your job is to continually get more and more out
of people—leads exactly and inexorably to the world depicted by the
Boston Globe. And the culprit? In Grove's words, as indeed in almost
all fast capitalist literature, the culprits are increased global competition
and advances in science and technology.

The reality of the new capitalism, thus far, is that a small number
of people have become 'big winners', a larger number of people have
seen their income decline or grow at an historically low rate, and an
even larger number of people are in or facing poverty. There is a certain
logic to the new capitalism. Initially two forces drive it: global competition and the fragmentation of mass markets. The globalization of
competition makes competition fiercer and makes losing all the more
likely. Science and technology allow the mass market to be fragmented
into many sub-markets, to which more and more competitors can direct
their efforts. However, with such smaller fragmented markets there is
less for each competitor to win (Madrick 1995).

Well, less for *most* competitors to win. There is a crucial winner-
take-all aspect to the new capitalism, which follows from the effects
of science and technology (Frank and Cook 1995). When local communities were fairly autonomous they could each have their own artists,
musicians, doctors, lawyers, professors, and so on. But today, as Rabo
Karabekian, the protagonist of Kurt Vonnegut's novel *Bluebeard*, says:

> . . . simply moderate giftedness has been made worthless by the
> printing press and radio and television and satellites and all that. A
> moderately gifted person who would have been a community
> treasure a thousand years ago has to give up, has to go into some
> other line of work, since modern communication has put him into
> daily competition with nothing but the world's champions. The
> entire planet can get along nicely with maybe a dozen champion
> performers in each area of human giftedness (Vonnegut 1987: 75,
> cited in Frank & Cook 1995: 1–2).

Why buy the recording of a local singer when you can buy the
'best' singer in the world for the same (or a lower) price? Why go to
the local college when you can as easily travel to the 'best' university?
Why trust the local lawyer, doctor, engineer, or agent when modern
information technology has let everyone know who the 'best' is and

you can hire them from afar and deal with them by fax and e-mail? Why hire local workers when there are cheaper and 'better' ones elsewhere who can do the work via computers and other space-fracturing technologies? Why buy the local brands when the 'best' can be shipped from Timbuktoo by this afternoon?

Even if the 'best' is only a little better than the 'next best', why settle for anything less, when it is as cheap and easy? Whence we get a small number of big winners ('the best') and a large number of losers (many of whom are nearly as good)—much as in running the hundred yard dash where the winner goes on to fame and fortune, though winning by only a hairsbreadth (and no one remembers the losers). Of course, this process has been going on for a long time, but it has greatly accelerated and will only intensify as modern technology shatters space and time further, putting, in any market, the very best—or at least the most 'hyped-up'— against everyone else.

The fierceness of competition, the fragmentation of markets, and the winner-take-all nature of our science-and-technology-driven world means that competition centers around two things: 'quality' (i.e. the 'best' product or service for the lowest price), and 'identity' (i.e., fitting the niche as perfectly as possible so as to gain customer loyalty). Competition around quality leads to constant innovation, lean and mean production, and less and less profit margin for most competitors, with large but often short-run profits for a few. Competition around identity means customization and the creation of a local, 'close to the customer' image on the part of big businesses which need desperately to please and retain customers.

But, as we have seen, the 'local' in the new capitalism is a deeply paradoxical notion. It is often the protective coloring taken on by very large and global corporations in different contexts. And, furthermore, the winner-take-all principle still operates in fractured niche markets (now we get the very best musical group for new age, religion-seeking baby-boomers, or the very best lawyer specializing in medium-size company takeovers in Southeast Asian countries).

Constant innovation, lean and mean efficiency, acceptance of high risk, and the meeting of intense customer demands create a need for smart and fully committed employees, each and every one of whom has to add value at every moment to the enterprise. Remember, in a winner-take-all market, finishing *near* the top can still spell disaster. Only a fanatically committed team can take the company over the top. The need for intense loyalty and commitment under such stressful conditions leads to the focus on enculturation, communities of practice, core values, and visionary leadership.

The competitors in the new capitalism are people, groups and tribes, companies and networks of companies, districts, counties or provinces, countries and regions. The same principles apply at all levels. Thus the cooperative in Nicaragua fails because one in El Salvador or Honduras succeeds; thus people in Los Angeles are forced into menial jobs with wages below the poverty line because workers in Japan find jobs as knowledge workers. Everything affects everything everywhere—hence the interest in, and relevance of, chaos theory and the notion of complex distributed systems.

In the new capitalism, both in theory (e.g. in fast capitalist texts) and in practice (e.g. in actual work sites of the sort we saw in Silicon Valley and Nicaragua), words are taking on new meaning, language and communication are being recruited for new ends and in the construction of new identities, multiple literacies are being distributed in new ways. And here there are possibilities for renewal, transformation, and struggle: possibilities for transmuting the new capitalism in to a new world that is not centered around consumers and markets. But we will have to delve and struggle for new meanings for words like 'best', 'quality', 'global', and 'local', as well as for a new morality for a new world.

We have argued in this book that the new work order makes us confront directly, at a fundamental level, the issue of goals and ends, of culture and core values, of the nature of language, learning, and literacy in and out of schools. We have seen that both a sociocultural approach to literacy and new-capitalist business argue that learning for performance requires the acquisition of tacit knowledge through immersion in communities of practice. We have seen, also, the need to go beyond simple immersion to gain the ability both to reflect on one's tacit knowledge and to critique the communities within which one has achieved it. We have seen as well, however, the perils and paradoxes of such critique in the new-capitalist workplace, as well as in classrooms.

For educators, then, a key task is to renew the basic question: 'What should we teach and learn, and why?' We want to close with a brief discussion of this question. Here too we have no definitive answers; our aim is to elaborate the issues in all their complexity.

II Goals and schools

The question of goals in schools has traditionally been answered in terms that place academic 'disciplinary' knowledge at the center of schooling. So let's consider for a moment the nature of academic disciplines and the sorts of goals that appear when academic knowledge is placed at the center of schooling, as it so often has been, at least for 'successful' students. This will allow us also to see how these goals can be transformed when academic knowledge is pushed from the center of attention, as is happening today, in many respects, under the influence of the new work order.

Consider the following four points that can be made about any academic discipline. For the sake of concreteness we will make them about physics, but any other area would do nearly as well. Physics, of course, has the added virtue that it carries the sorts of technical knowledge so highly valued in the new capitalism:

1. Physicists think about what they think about—things like force and motion—in certain ways, quite different ways from those we use in our everyday lives.

2. Physics has certain 'products' and 'results', things like laws, equations, algorithms, principles, and technologies that can be used to solve certain sorts of problems inside and outside the domain of physics proper. One can use these without having the same mental representations in one's head that a physicist has, much as one can use certain tools of carpentry without having a professional carpenter's knowledge and skills.

3. Physicists construct (develop, transform, and distribute) their knowledge through certain social and rhetorical processes. They actually engage in certain social practices—actually *do* their work in certain ways—that are hidden in their journal articles and effaced in their public presentations, which tend to emphasise the cognitive aspects of their work against the social and rhetorical.

4. Physicists' knowledge has developed historically in relationship to and in contrast with other ways of thinking, doing, and knowing, including other specialized ways and our everyday ways. This, too, tends to get effaced when physicists write and give public presentations—in fact, they tend to treat history as irrelevant, merely a record of 'errors' leading to today's 'truth'.

Current educational reform proposals, if and when they retain academic knowledge as the center of schooling, tend to emphasize one or more of these points, often, of course, in relation to the age and setting of the learners. These four points represent four 'focus points' in regard to the question of *what* should be taught and learned. As we see below, although they are formulated in terms of academic disciplines, they also represent four focus points for educational goals that move away from academic knowledge and academic disciplines as the center of education.

Focus 1: Thinking: mental representations. Here we are concerned with what's in the head. We want learners to gain the sorts of mental representations that members of academic disciplines have in their heads. For example, 'force', 'work', and 'motion' are understood in quite specific ways by physicists, ways that are quite different from the everyday understandings of these terms. From this focus point, education is centrally about achieving such understandings, though not necessarily through engaging in the full gamut of the discipline's social and rhetorical practices. Using well-structured materials we guide students through problems so that they come to see and confront the difference between their everyday way of seeing things and the specialist way. Eventually they are to come to see and cut up the world in the way in which the expert does, at least while working on problems in the domain.

Focus 2: Tools: products. Traditional education is focused on getting learners to remember and be able to reproduce on tests the 'facts' and 'results' of the academic disciplines. It is precisely this approach that leads to the lack of 'real understanding' so bemoaned by the cognitive scientists (see Chapter 3). However, a more contemporary approach stresses the ability of individuals or, better yet, groups (teams) of students to discover and use the knowledge-handling tools associated with academic disciplines (whether tools associated with a given discipline or tools used across several). Students need not think like academics, nor need they engage in the social and rhetorical practices typical of any given discipline whose tools they are using. For example, time versus distance graphs and speed versus velocity graphs are tools used by physicists. We can give students lots of data on the speeds, distances, and times of moving objects (e.g. cars) and, using various material and computational aids, *let them produce* time versus distance graphs and speed versus velocity graphs. They can then go on to use such graphs to work on a variety of problems, not necessarily those found typically in physics but, perhaps, in the world of work. Here we pay less attention to what is in learners' heads, and more to the ways in which they can produce results, especially in collaboration with others. Of course, Focus 1 should lead to similar results; this second focus simply cares less about the ways of thinking characteristic of a discipline and more about the ability to use 'tools' to do things.

Focus 3: Culture: Discourse. Here we attempt to produce a community of practice that bears some similarity to the valued or positive parts of an academic Discourse, while downplaying the technical aspects of its content and practices. Students learn how to handle knowledge and language in ways that are like those in academic disciplines. The stress here is not on what is 'in the head' but on interactive social-rhetorical practices. These practices are meant to constitute a Discourse of learners and knowers working on content that is related to that of an academic Discourse, in social and rhetorical ways that are akin to disciplines, but rendered relevant and suitable for a particular community of learners. We saw an example of such a pedagogy in Chapter 3 when we discussed the work of Ann Brown and Joe Campione at the University of California at Berkeley.

Focus 4: Critique: meta-understanding. Here the history, philosophy, and sociology of knowledge-building are central. The goal is to understand how different Discourses—e.g. physics and biology—have been built in history through various (and different) ways of thinking, acting, interacting, talking, and writing in certain places and with characteristic props (objects, tools, technologies, and so forth). The goal is also to understand how various specialist Discourses relate to and conflict with various everyday Discourses, as well as to various public sphere and global Discourses connected to government, business, religion, and the like. Students may not actually think like a physicist in solving problems, they may not be able to build or use the products of physicists, and they may not be in a community that acts, talks, and writes like physicists. They will, however, see all of these things as objects for meta-level understanding. Such students are 'philosophers- historians-ethnographers-sociologists' of knowledge in institutions and in society as a whole.

Obviously, each one of these focuses will to some extent involve the others. Ideally, most school reformers want to achieve all four, though usually they emphasize one or another. Figure 2 encapsulates these focuses for educational goals.

Figure 2: Four focuses for educational goals

1. THINKING	2. TOOLS
3. DISCOURSE	4. CRITIQUE

It is obvious that there are important interrelations among Focuses 1–4, and much educational research and controversy centers on trying to tease out just what these relationships are. For example, there are those who believe that 3 (creating a Discourse) will lead to 1 (thinking like a physicist) which will in turn lead to 2 (being able to use technical tools to produce results). Others, however, believe that anything approaching a Discourse that could, in fact, lead to 1 is not sustainable in typical classrooms, and that there are other and better ways to achieve 1 more directly—often, these days, using computers as pedagogical aids (Papert 1993). Then again one could claim that in the world of work outside of schools it matters very little what is *in* your head, and it rarely matters whether you actually think like a disciplinary expert unless you actually are one. What really matters is what you can *do* and how you can do it *with others*, a version of focus 2. This in turn leads to the question of why we should bother to assess individuals and what's in their heads. Why not assess what people can achieve collaboratively with others in the way of using tools and techniques to produce results and solve problems relevant to work and our increasingly complex everyday world? (Bereiter 1994). After all, it might be claimed, that's how things work *outside* school.

It is a particularly interesting question—and a poorly studied one—as to how one achieves 4 (Meta-understanding; Critique of Discourses). For example, it might be argued that the experience of engaging in 3 (a disciplinary Discourse) is necessary for engagement in 4—perhaps, even, 1, 2 and 3 are all necessary for engagement in 4. But then again many people have achieved insightful meta-knowledge of the workings of the sciences (for example), without being enculturated into them very deeply or without being able to use the tools to master very advanced problems. And vice versa: many people have achieved great mastery of science without achieving any very profound meta-knowledge or critique of their own or other disciplines. Certainly 4 requires 'confrontation' (in a variety of senses) with Discourses, but exactly of what sort is still very much an open and crucial question.

These comments are meant merely to give a sense of the sorts of controversies that can arise when we consider any one of the above focuses in relation to the others. While might we say that we would like to achieve all four focuses with all learners, the reality is that usually we must place our emphasis and our main efforts in one area or another. Workers in cognitive science have tended to emphasize 1 (Thinking) and/or 2 (Tools), while those in sociocultural literacy have tended to gravitate toward 3 (Discourse) and/or 4 (Critique). Of late there is some convergence of the two areas, cognitive science and sociocultural literacy, around 3 (Discourse), thanks to the work of Ann Brown and her colleagues, work that we discussed in Chapter 3. In

Australia, the well-known 'genre movement' (see e.g. Christie 1990; Cope & Kalantzis 1993) has stressed 2 (Tools) with a particular emphasis on language tools (for science, see Halliday & Martin 1993).

In the terms in which we discussed them above, these four focuses all give a certain pride of place to academic knowledge. At the same time, however, they allow us very easily to construct key goals in a way that refrains from placing academic disciplines at the center of education. Academic disciplines are but one large class of Discourses amongst many others. If we substitute for them, say, Discourses connected to work, or to the public sphere more generally (e.g. government), we can get goals that stress thinking like members of those Discourses, using tools from them, engaging in social practices akin to theirs, and critiquing those Discourses in relation to others.

Let us turn, then, to a view of education in which academic knowledge and academic disciplines are not at the center, however much they have been at the center of our discussion so far. There are, in fact, two broad classes of educational goals. One centers on academic disciplines. These are the goals usually promulgated by university academics. The other class displaces academic knowledge from pride of place, replacing it with a variety of other focuses, often in the world of work, experience, or the public sphere. Such goals are often promulgated by those with connections to the world outside the university, for example, those with connections to the business world.

In the context of claims about a new work order of the sort we have discussed throughout this book, the discussion of educational goals takes on a very different flavor from the academic one. Given the central role of technology, technological innovation, and technical skills in the new capitalism, many proponents stress focus 2 (Tools); that is, being able to use the technical tools of academic disciplines, but 'on site' in the actual contexts of work. They also stress the need to change people's values and attitudes so as to deal with the tensions and demands of this new world. Thus, too, they tend to stress a version of 3 (Discourse); that is, creating a Discourse in the classroom and school, but a Discourse that 'fits' the values and norms of the new work order, not academic disciplines. For example, if children come to accept that the 'freedom' to be an empowered worker/partner is limited by the need to accept the goals, visions, and core values of the new capitalism, then what we have called in this book the core paradox of the new capitalism will be 'resolved' or better put, perhaps, buried.

However, new-capitalist educational reformers also have versions of 1 (Thinking) and 4 (Critique). In the case of 1, they stress not the need for the mental representations of disciplinary experts but, rather, the sorts of thinking skills that allow one to be an 'expert novice' (Bruer 1993: Ch. 3; Bereiter and Scardamalia 1993)—that is, someone expert at continually learning anew and in depth. Not all disciplinary experts are, in fact, good at this, though some are (at mastering, for example, new fields and disciplines, using their prior knowledge as a bridge).

Finally, in the case of focus 4, the new capitalists stress that, thanks to technological and global changes, contemporary organizations and the contemporary world are composed of incredibly complex systems (Senge 1991; Senge et al. 1994). People and organizations are linked in ever more intricate and complex ways. The acts of each person in a complex system have effects that quickly ramify far away from that person in time and space, effects that are often unknown and unintended. What looks 'rational' from the local perspective of one person in a complex system may, given its wider consequences be deeply detrimental to the system as a whole. Thus it is crucial that all workers, managers, and leaders in these systems understand their place in the system and the workings of the system as a whole, as well as its interrelations with other complex systems. This is a 'systems' version of the sort of meta-knowledge required in focus 4.

Figure 3 summarizes the new-capitalist form of the four focuses.

Figure 3: Four focuses for educational goals, new-capitalist version

1. THINKING LIKE AN 'EXPERT NOVICE'	2. TECHNICAL AND COMMUNICATION TOOLS USEABLE ON SITE
3. DISCOURSE BASED ON CORE NORMS AND VALUES OF THE NEW CAPITALISM	4. SYSTEMS UNDERSTANDING

The new-capitalist educators stress education and learning as a lifelong enterprise, and thus do not concentrate only on children and schools. But they tend to stress one or the other of their four focuses, often varying with the context. With respect to schools, for instance, many stress the achievement of 1 (Thinking like an 'Expert Novice') through classrooms and schools set up under the guidelines of 3 (Discourse attuned to the new capitalism). Such classrooms and schools are themselves complex systems, and so can lead to the beginnings of 4 (Systems Understanding) as well. In addition, 2 (Tools) and 4

(Systems Understanding) are to be picked up in actual practices, on site and on demand, both in classrooms, and in the life-long and often 'self-directed' learning that people who achieve 1 (Thinking Like an Expert Novice) do throughout their lives.

Ideologically, the dominant goal throughout is usually 1, although in actual practice 2 and 3 tend to be stressed for lower-level worker/partners. Finally, the new-capitalist version of 4 tends to value critique as a form of creativity leading to the re-engineering of old processes and structures, and the creating of new ones, but limited by an acceptance of new-capitalist values.

The new-capitalist reformer places the world of work at the center of education, not in any old-fashioned sense of 'job skills', but in terms of learning to learn, mastering technical tools, and understanding complex systems. From this standpoint, education would be organized not around disciplinary titles, like 'physics' or 'literature', but around themes, systems, problems, and/or sites. As universities and academic disciplines themselves are reorganized by the new capitalism, there may well be increasing convergence in these matters, a process already in motion.

Learning and working are conflating more and more, both because learning is more and more out of sync and out of date when it is off site, and because work changes so quickly that *learning* a job and *doing* a job are often practically synonymous. We have argued that in such a world learning and working are both primarily about the formation of social identities ('kinds of people'), with their concomitant values, within what we have called Discourses. This brings us to what we see as the possibilities in our new world.

Seeing the new capitalism for what it is—namely a new Discourse in the making—allows us to juxtapose it with other, competing, over-lapping, and mutually adjusting Discourses, such as a critical version of sociocultural literacy (which has informed the critique in this book), the various Discourses of school reform, and a variety of other community-based and public-sphere Discourses. Further, we have argued that there are complex processes of alignment, sometimes in words and sometimes in deeds as well, among the new capitalism and other Discourses. Such juxtaposing of Discourses—which involves juxta-posing different, 'kinds of people', often people inhabiting the one body—allows us also to envision other, alternative goals of schooling and learning, based on a new Discourse which is opposed, at various points, to the Discourse of the new capitalism.

This new Discourse would disavow the consumer determinism of the new capitalism. It would argue for the reinvigoration of the local as against the *'faux'* local of the new capitalism. It would see critique as necessary to real learning and thus as part and parcel of critical thinking and the empowerment of workers. Most importantly, it would envision a new 'global citizenship' in terms of which we all begin to care about the members of the cooperative in Nicaragua *and* about the poor in our own communities—as being linked to each other and ourselves—if only to avoid degradation of *all* our spaces and lives.

But then this can only happen when the newly emerging Discourse of the new capitalism, including its various textual representations as well as its situated unfolding in real workplaces, becomes central to *all* education. This can be done by juxtaposing the Discourse of the new capitalism, and its many variants, with other Discourses; by placing it within a 'Discourse map' of our societies and the world. In our new 'knowledge world', learning and education become always and everywhere about being in, about comparing and contrasting, reflecting on and critiquing, *Discourses*—about the *kinds* of people we are, are becoming, and want to be. That is the discussion and the educational project that this book is intended to stimulate and promote.

In *The Vision of the Anointed* (1995) Thomas Sowell, a senior fellow at the Hoover Institution, a well-known 'right wing' thinktank, contrasts what he calls The Tragic Vision, which he associates with 'conservatives', with the Vision of the Anointed, which he associates with 'liberals' and those on the 'left'. Sowell claims that those with the tragic vision see humans as inherently morally and epistemologically limited, and see social outcomes as being largely the result of massive tradeoffs and complex interactions within complex systems—whether markets, legal systems, work systems, or international relations. They see the act of intervening in these systems as being inherently risky. On the other hand, Sowell argues that those with the vision of the anointed see human capability as unlimited but in need of manipulation by the social policies, planning, and interventions of those with the 'right' social conscience (i.e. themselves). Those with the vision of the anointed see social outcomes as resulting from people's deliberate actions and dispositions (e.g. racism, power-seeking, greed, etc.), not from the complex workings of historically evolved systems that reflect the 'wisdom', interests, and compromises of vast multitudes of people.

Sowell almost certainly would place us among those with the vision of the anointed. But we are acutely aware that no one has anointed us, and that we have no all-encompassing vision or definitive solutions. We most certainly do not think that we know better than other people what is 'moral' or 'in their best interests'. Since we take a sociocultural and historical view of language and meaning, we do not think that all social outcomes are rooted in individual thoughts and dispositions. In fact, we have argued throughout this book that the new work order is the outcome of very complex forces, forces which have specific consequences for the 'winners' and for the 'losers'—and, indeed, as the French Industry Minister reminds us, the consequences for the 'losers' may eventually impact greatly on the consequences for the 'winners'.

Sowell ignores the fact that many of those with the tragic vision are reluctant to engage in social reform because the current systems, by and large, advantage them. Be that as it may, we do not advocate the inculcating of people with *our* politics (or anyone else's in particular) as a solution to the world's ills. Rather, we advocate letting them, at work and at school, gain a deep understanding of the workings of Discourses in society. This understanding may, indeed, unmask greed and manipulation hiding behind systems and their assorted rationalizations. But we would argue that it will also make for better knowledge workers *and* a more just social order, not merely because people will have listened to the recounting of a vision such as that portrayed in this book, but because they will have broadened their own frame of reference to encompass both the complex systems and the specific acts that shape and transform their lives in our global world. Seeing a Discourse map of a society offers a chance to see the many paths running through time and space, a chance to see the others who, at this time and place, share our 'paths through life' (Shuman 1992), a chance to elect to join the paths of others—if only for a while—and, should history, fortune, and the gods permit, a chance to forge new paths.

Bibliography

Aronowitz, S. and DiFazio, W. (1994). *The jobless future: Sci-tech and the dogma of work*. Minneapolis: University of Minnesota Press

Aronson, E. (1978). *The jigsaw classroom*. Beverly Hills, Cal.: Sage

Bailey, J. (1988). *Pessimism*. London: Routledge

Bakhtin, M. (1984). *Rabelais and his world*. Indiana: Indiana University Press

Barnet, R. J. and Cavanagh, J. (1994). *Global dreams: Imperial corporations and the new world order*. New York: Simon and Schuster

Barsalou, L. W. (1992). *Cognitive psychology: An overview for cognitive scientists*. Hillsdale, N. J.: Lawrence Erlbaum

Baudrillard, J. (1988). *America*. Trans. by C. Turner. London: Verso

Bauman, Z. (1992). *Intimations of postmodernity*. London: Routledge

——(1995). *Life in fragments: essays in postmodern morality*. Oxford: Basil Blackwell

Bennis, W., Parikh, J., and Lessem, R. (1994). *Beyond leadership: Balancing economics, ethics and ecology*. Oxford: Basil Blackwell

Bereiter, C. (1994). 'Constructivism, socioculturalism, and Popper's World 3', *Educational Researcher*, 23: 21–23

Bereiter, C. and Scardamalia, M. (1993). *Surpassing ourselves: An inquiry into the nature and implications of expertise*. Chicago: Open Court

Best, M. (1990). *The new competition: Institutions of industrial restructuring*. Cambridge, Mass.: Harvard University Press

Best, S. and Kellner, D. (1991). *Postmodern theory*. New York: Guilford

Bizzell, P. (1992). *Academic discourse and critical consciousness*. Pittsburgh: University of Pittsburgh Press

Block, F. (1990). *Postindustrial possibilities*. Berkeley and Los Angeles: University of California Press

Bloome, D. and Green, J. (1991). 'Educational contexts of literacy', in W. Grabe, ed., *Annual Review of Applied Linguistics*, 12: 49–70

Boden, D. (1994). *The business of talk: Organizations in action*. Cambridge: Polity Press

Bourdieu, P. (1979/1984). *Distinction: A social critique of the judgement of taste*. Cambridge, Mass.: Harvard University Press

——(1991). *Language and symbolic power*. Cambridge, Mass.: Harvard University Press

Boyett, J. H. and Conn, H. P. (1992). *Workplace 2000: The revolution reshaping American business*. New York: Plume/Penguin

Brandt, W. /Independent commission on international development issues, (1980). *North–South: A Programme for Survival*. London: Pan Books

Brown, A. L. (1994). 'The advancement of learning', *Educational Researcher* 23: 4–12

Brown, A. L. and Palincsar, A. S. (1989). 'Guided, cooperative learning and individual knowledge acquisition', in L. B. Resnick, ed., *Knowing, learning, and instruction: Essays in honor of Robert Glaser*. Hillsdale, N.J.: Lawrence Erlbaum, 393–451

Brown, A. L., Ash, D., Rutherford, M., Nakagawa, K., Gordon, A., and Campione, J. (1993). 'Distributed expertise in the classroom', in G. Salomon, ed., *Distributed cognitions: Psychological and educational considerations*. New York: Cambridge University Press, 188–228

Bruer, J. T. (1993). *Schools for thought: A science of learning in the classroom*. Cambridge, Mass.: MIT Press

Cardoso, F.H. (1993). 'North–South relations in the present context: A new dependency?', in M. Carnoy, M. Castells, S. Cohen and F.M. Cardoso, *The new global economy in the information age: Reflections on our changing world*. University Park, Penn.: Pennsylvania State University Press, 149–59

Carnoy, M., Castells, M., Cohen, S. and Cardoso, F.M., (1993). *The new global economy in the information age: Reflections on our changing world*. University Park, Penn.: Pennsylvania State University Press

Carnoy, M. and Samoff, J. (1990). *Education and social transition in the third world*. Princeton, N.J.: Princeton University Press

Castells, M. (1993). 'The informational economy and the new international division of labor', in M. Carnoy, M. Castells, S. Cohen and F.M. Cardoso, *The new global economy in the information age: Reflections on our changing world*. University Park, Penn.: Pennsylvania State University Press, 15–43

Cazden, C. (1981). 'Performance before competence: Assistance to child discourse in the zone of proximal development', *Quarterly Newsletter of the Laboratory of Comparative Human Cognition*, 3: 5–8

Champy, J. (1995). *Reeingineering management: The mandate for new leadership*. New York: Harper Business

Christie, F., ed. (1990). *Literacy for a changing world*. Melbourne: Australian Council for Educational Research

Clark, K. and Holquist, M. (1984). *Mikhail Bakhtin*. Cambridge, Mass.: Harvard University Press

Cohen, S. and Zysman, J. (1987). *Manufacturing matters: The myth of the post-industrial economy*. New York: Basic Books

Collins, J. C. and Porras, J. I. (1994). *Built to last: Successful habits of visonary companies*. New York: Harper Business

Cope, B. and Kalantzis, M., eds (1993). *The powers of literacy: A genre approach to teaching writing*. Pittsburgh: University of Pittsburgh Press

Crosby, P. B. (1979). *Quality is free: The art of making quality certain*. New York: McGraw-Hill

——(1994). *Completeness: Quality for the 21st century*. New York: Plume (orig. New York: Dutton, 1992)

Cross, K. F., Feather, J. J. and Lynch, R. L. (1994). *Corporate renaissance: The art of reengineering*. Oxford: Basil Blackwell

Davidow, W. and Malone, M. (1992). *The virtual corporation: Structuring and revitalizing the corporation for the 21st century*. New York: Harper

Delpit, L. (1995). *Other people's children: Cultural conflict in the classroom*. New York: The New Press

Derrida, J. (1976). *Of grammatology*. Trans. by Gayatri Chakravorty Spivak. Baltimore: Johns Hopkins University Press

Dobyns, L. and Crawford-Mason, C. (1991). *Quality or else: The revolution in world business*. Boston: Houghton Mifflin

Drucker, P. F. (1993). *Post-capitalist society*. New York: Harper

Edwards, D. and Mercer, N. (1987). *Common knowledge: The development of understanding in the classroom*. London: Methuen

Foucault, M. (1980). *Power/knowledge: Selected interviews and other writings 1972–1977*. Edited by C. Gordon, L. Marshall, J. Meplam and K. Soper. Brighton, Sussex: The Harvester Press

Frank, A. G. (1967). *Capitalism and underdevelopment in Latin America*. New York and London: Monthly Review Press

Frank, R. H. and Cook, P. J. (1995). *The winner-take-all society*. New York: The Free Press

Freire, P. (1970). *Pedagogy of the oppressed*. Trans. M.B. Ramos. New York: Seabury Press

Galeano, E. (1973). *Open veins of Latin America: Five centuries of the pillage of a continent*. New York: Monthly Review Press

Gardner, H. (1985). *The mind's new science*. New York: Basic Books

——(1991). *The unschooled mind: How children think and how schools should teach*. New York: Basic Books

Garton, A. and Pratt, C. (1989). *Learning to be literate: The development of spoken and written language*. Oxford: Basil Blackwell

Gee, J. P. (1989). 'Literacies and traditions', *Journal of Education*, 171: 26–38

——(1992). *The social mind*. New York: Bergin and Garvey

——(1993). 'Quality, science, and the lifeworld: The alignment of business and education', *Critical Forum*, 2: 3–13

——(1994). 'New alignments and old literacies: Critical literacy, postmodernism, and fast capitalism', in P. O'Connor, ed., *Thinking work, vol. 1: Theoretical perspectives on workers' literacies*. Sydney: ALBSAC

——(1996). *Social linguistics and literacies: Ideology in Discourses*, second edition. London: Falmer Press (first edition 1990)

Gee, J. P. and Lankshear, C. (1995). 'The new work order: Critical language awareness and "fast capitalist" texts', *Discourse*, 16: 5–19

Gopen, G. D. (1984). 'Rhyme and reason: Why the study of poetry is the best preparation for the study of law', *College English*, 46: 333–47

Graff, H. J. (1987). *The legacies of literacy: Continuities and contradictions in Western culture and society*. Bloomington, Ind.: Indiana University Press

Habermas, J. (1984). *Theory of communicative action*, vol. 1. Trans. by T. McCarthy. London: Heinemann

Hacking, I. (1986). 'Making up people', in T. C. Heller, M. Sosna and D. E. Wellbery (with A. I. Davidson, A. Swidler and I. Watt), eds, *Reconstructing individualism: Autonomy, individuality, and the self in Western thought*. Stanford: Stanford University Press, 222–36

——(1994). 'The looping effects of human kinds', in D. Sperber, D. Premack and A. J. Premack, eds, *Causal cognition: A multidisciplinary approach*. Oxford: Clarendon Press

Halliday, M. A. K. and Martin, J. R. (1993). *Writing science: Literacy and discursive power*. Pittsburgh: University of Pittsburgh Press

Hamel, G. and Prahalad, C. K. (1994). *Competing for the future: Breakthrough strategies for seizing control of your industry and creating the markets of tomorrow*. Boston, Mass.: Harvard Business School Press

Hammer, M. and Champy, J. (1993). *Reengineering the corporation: A manifesto for business revolution*. New York: Harper Business

Handy, C. (1989). *The age of unreason*. London: Business Books

——(1994). *The age of paradox*. Boston: Harvard Business School Press

Heath, S. B. (1983). *Ways with words: Language, life, and work in communities and classrooms*. Cambridge: Cambridge University Press

Howard, R. (1984). 'High technology and the reenchantment of the work place', *National Productivity Review*, Summer

Hutchins, E. (1995). *Cognition in the wild*. Cambridge, Mass.: MIT Press

Imparato, N. and Harari, O. (1994). *Jumping the curve: Innovation and strategic choice in an age of transition*. San Francisco: Jossey-Bass

John-Steiner, V., Panofsky, C. P., and Smith, L. W., eds (1994). *Sociocultural approaches to language and literacy*. Cambridge: Cambridge University Press

Kauffman, S. A. (1991). *Origins of order: Self-organization and selection in evolution*. Oxford: Oxford University Press

Kelly, K. (1994). *Out of control: The new biology of machines, social systems, and the economic world*. Reading, Mass.: Addison-Wesley

Kennedy, P. (1993). *Preparing for the twenty-first century*. New York: Random House

Kotter, J. P. (1995). *The new rules: How to succeed in today's post-corporate world*. New York: The Free Press

Kress, G. (1985). *Linguistic processes in sociocultural practice*. Oxford: Oxford University Press

Lafontaine, O. (1990). 'El socialismo y los nuevos movimientos sociales', *El Socialismo del Futuro*, 1, May

Lankshear, C. with Lawler, M. (1987). *Literacy, schooling, and revolution*. London: Falmer

Lash, S. and Urry, J. (1994). *Economies of signs and space*. London: Sage

Lave, J. (1988). *Cognition in practice: Mind, mathematics and culture in everyday life*. Cambridge: Cambridge University Press

Lave, J. and Wenger, E. (1991). *Situated learning: Legitimate peripheral participation*. New York: Cambridge University Press

Leach, W. (1993). *Land of desire: Merchants, power, and the rise of a new American culture*. New York: Vintage

Levett, A. and Lankshear, C. (1994). 'Literacies, workplaces and the demands of new times', in M. Brown, ed., *Literacies and the workplace: A collection of original essays*. Geelong: Deakin University Press

Lipnack, J. and Stamps, J. (1993). *The team net factor: Bringing the power of boundary crossing into the heart of your business*. Essex Junction, Vt.: Oliver Wright

Lorentz, E. N. (1993). *The essence of chaos*. Seattle: University of Washington Press

Lyotard, J-F. (1988). *Le postmoderne explique aux enfants: Correspondance 1982–1985*. Paris: Galilee

Madrick, J. (1995). *The end of affluence: The causes and consequences of America's economic decline*. New York: Random House

Minnis, M. (1994). 'Toward a definition of law school readiness', in V. John-Steiner, C. P. Panofsky, and L. W. Smith, eds, *Sociocultural approaches to language and literacy: An interactionist perspective*. Cambridge: Cambridge University Press, 347–90

Newman, D., Griffin, P. and Cole, M. (1989). *The construction zone*. Cambridge: Cambridge University Press

Nonaka, I. and Takeuchi, H. (1995). *The knowledge-creating company: How Japanese companies create the dynamics of innovation*. New York: Oxford University Press

O'Connor, P. (1993). 'Crossing the borders of workers' literacy', *Focus: Occasional Papers in Adult Basic Education*, No. 3. Sydney: ALBSAC

Papert, S. (1993). *The children's machine: Rethinking school in the age of the computer*. New York: Basic Books

Parker, R. E. (1994). *Flesh peddlers and warm bodies: The temporary help industry and its workers*. New Brunswick, N.J.: Rutgers University Press

Perelman, L. J. (1992). *School's out: Hyperlearning, the new technology, and the end of education.* New York: William Morrow

Perkins, D. (1992). *Smart schools: From training memories to educating minds.* New York: The Free Press

——(1995). *Outsmarting IQ: The emerging science of learnable intelligence.* New York: The Free Press

Peters, T. (1992). *Liberation management: Necessary disorganization for the nanosecond nineties.* New York; Fawcett

——(1994). *The Tom Peters seminar: Crazy times call for crazy organizations.* New York: Vintage Books

Reich, R. B. (1992). *The work of nations.* New York: Vintage Books

Rogoff, B. (1990). *Apprenticeship in thinking.* New York: Oxford University Press

Rushkoff, D. (1994). *Media virus!: Hidden agendas in popular culture.* New York: Ballantine Books

Sashkin, M. and Kiser, K. J. (1993). *Putting total quality management to work.* San Francisco: Berrett-Koehler

Saxenian, A. (1994) *Regional Advantage: Culture and competition in Silicon Valley and Route 128.* Cambridge, Mass: Harvard University Press

Scollon, R. and Scollon, S. W. (1981). *Narrative, literacy, and face in interethnic communication.* Norwood, N.J.: Ablex

Senge, P. M. (1991). *The fifth discipline: The art and practice of the learning organization.* New York: Doubleday

Senge, P. M., Roberts, C., Ross, R. B., Smith B. J. and Kline, A. (1994). *The fifth discipline fieldbook: Strategies and tools for building a learning organization.* New York: Doubleday

Shuman, A. (1992). 'Literacy: Local uses and global perspectives', presentation to the Literacies Institute, Newton, Massachusetts, January

Siegel, L. (1993) New chips in old skins: Work, labor and Silicon Valley. Excerpts from a talk. In M. Stack and J. Davies, eds, CPU, electronic bulletin board

Smith, H. (1995). *Rethinking America: A new game plan from the American innovators: Schools, business, people, work.* New York: Random House

Street, B. (1984). *Literacy in theory and practice.* Cambridge: Cambridge University Press

Sowell, T. (1995). *The vision of the anointed: Self-congratulation as a basis for social policy.* New York: Basic Books

Taylor, M. C. and Saarinen, E. (1994). *Imagologies: Media philosophy.* London: Routledge

Thurow, L. (1992). *Head to head: The coming economic battle among Japan, Europe and America.* New York: Morrow

Vilas, C. (1989). *State, class, and ethnicity in Nicaragua.* Boulder: Lynne Rienner Publishers

Vonnegut, K. (1987). *Bluebeard.* New York: Delacorte Press

Vygotsky, L. S. (1978). *Mind in society: The development of higher psycho-logical processes*. Cambridge, Mass.: Harvard University Press

Waldrop, M. M. (1992). *Complexity: The emerging science at the edge of order and chaos*. New York: Simon & Schuster

White, J. B. (1984). 'The judicial opinion and the poem: Ways of reading, ways of life', *Michigan Law Review*, 82: 1669–99

Wiggenhorn, W. (1990). 'Motorola U: When training becomes an education', *Harvard Business Review*, July–August, 71–83

Index

James Paul Gee is Jacob Hiatt Professor of Education in the Hiatt Centre at Clark University, Worcester, Massachusetts, and has published widely on education theory, discourse studies and linguistics; his writing includes *Social Linguistics* and *The Social Mind*.

Glynda Hull is Associate Professor of Language and Literacy Education at the University of California, Berkeley and Director of the College Writing Programs. She is editor of *Changing Work, Changing Workers*.

Colin Lankshear is Professor in the School of Language and Literacy Education at Queensland University of Technology. He is the author of *Literacy, Schooling and Revolution* and co-author of *Counternarratives*.

LaVergne, TN USA
11 March 2010

175717LV00001B/41/A